Pra

"MACK MALONEY'S F.

"Mack checks the Universe's ... and finds it's two quarts low!" —*Al Renaldo*, UFO Mechanic

"If ETs can tune into terrestrial radio, they'd better listen to Mack's show!" —*Pistol Pete Falconi*

"Mack gives the Universe a squirt of seltzer in the face…" —*Dribbles*, the Psychic Clown

"I'll be reading this book while I'm waiting for you in the parking lot…" —*The Black-Eyed Kid*

"Mack slices into the Cosmic Pizza with wit – and without the mushrooms!"—Switchblade *Steve Ward*

"Hemingway, Tolstoy, Steinbeck… and Mack!"
—*Emily M.*

"Even if I could comment on Mack's book, I have no comment…" —*Agent X*

"Mack's book is full of (bleep), (bleep) and (bleep). I highly recommend it to anyone who's into (bleep)!"
—*Jeff Lawrence*, MMMX-Files show editor & censor

"Mack's writing will knock you out faster than a sock full of nickels…" —*Willy Clubb*, MMMX-Files security chief

"Whenever I'm tempted to navel gaze, I read Mack's book instead!" —*No Belly Button Man*

"If you hear a droning noise in your head, read this book and it will go away!" —*Cindy Bailey Dove*, drone expert

MACK MALONEY'S
HAUNTED UNIVERSE

Books by Mack Maloney

Starhawk *series*
Starhawk
Planet America
The Fourth Empire
Battle at Zero Point
Storm Over Saturn

Chopper Ops *series*
Chopper Ops
Zero Red
Shuttle Down

Strikemasters *series*
Strikemasters
Rogue War
Fulcrum

Storm Birds *series*
Desert Lightning
Thunder from Heaven
The Gathering Storm

Iron Star
Thunder Alley

MACK MALONEY'S
HAUNTED UNIVERSE

Mack Maloney

Speaking Volumes, LLC
Naples, Florida
2018

Mack Maloney's Haunted Universe

Copyright © 2018 by Mack Maloney

Edited by Marc Zappulla

ISBN 978-1-62815-898-4

For Lois Lane

<u>Acknowledgements</u>

Many thanks to Juan-Juan and Commander Cobra, Pete Falconi, Jeff Lawrence and everyone at Port Broadcasting. Added thanks to Marc Zappulla, Phil Yebba, Agent X, Cindy Bailey Dove, Barry Keefe, Barry Wenig, Al Romano, Steve Ward and Emily Mittermaier. Special thanks to Gary Olsen, Larry Stone and Mike Robinson.

Very special thanks to all the guests and to our many fans and friends who listen to Mack Maloney's Military X-Files show.

Introduction

My first job out of college was as a sportswriter for a small newspaper on Boston's North Shore. Arriving at work at 4:45 AM, I would "rip" the United Press International news stories that had arrived via teletype during the night. National, international, and regional stories all went in their respective baskets. I took the sports stories and passed entertainment articles on to the Arts section people.

Every day UPI would also transmit three "Weird but True" stories that newspapers could use for filler. Most were very strange. A pig eats a baby in Mexico. The fourth most common name in China is "Ding." Most horns in U.S.-made cars beep in the key of F.

No one at our newspaper ever used these stories, so I started collecting them — and I've been collecting weird stories ever since.

This habit paid off when I was hired by Ted Turner's truTV to write for its web page "Conspiratorium." I would find ten to fifteen unusual stories every month that the web editors would then illustrate with photos. Some of what you'll read in these pages comes from that research, plus the stacks of notes I saved while writing two UFO-related books, "UFOs in Wartime," and "Beyond Area 51," as well as from my ongoing weird story file.

All of this stuff is fascinating to me, especially odd stories that have a military angle.

The inspiration for the title of this book came from a documentary I watched about alternate universes. Many astrophysicists now believe our universe is just one of an infinite number of universes that exist in close proximity to each other like bubbles in a handful of suds.

My first thought was, how strange it must be to exist in a universe that's alternate to our own. But on further thought, I wondered what if there was a chance that everything works perfectly in our alternate universes. Maybe everyone gets along, there's no war, no poverty, no greed, no racism, no fouling of our planet. Maybe nothing strange ever happens in those other places. Maybe everything can be explained, there are no mysteries, no paranormal and nothing ever goes bump in the night.

On the other hand, we live a weird existence, strange things happen here all the time, and we just take it for granted that's how things are.

But what if our existence is the anomaly?

What if we're the ones who live in the Haunted Universe?

—Mack Maloney

Foreword by Juan-Juan

I've known Mack for many years. I first met him when he needed someone to quickly "sanitize" his home computer. I became his technology adviser, and next thing I knew, I was co-hosting "Mack Maloney's Military X-Files" radio show.

As you probably know, Mack has authored many books. Two of my favorite titles are "UFOs in Wartime" and "Beyond Area 51." When you read them, as I will someday, I'm sure you will be both entertained and informed, probably beyond your wildest imagination. I'm told the material is witty as well as factual, so you don't feel you're being lectured to, like I did all through high school and college. God, higher education can be *so* boring!

Anyway, now comes "Mack Maloney's Haunted Universe," and I'll hazard a guess that it's Mack at his best. In fact, when I got this book, I was more excited than when I received all of the Beatles' remastered albums on vinyl, and *almost* as excited as when Nancy Wilson of Heart asked me to go on tour with the band as her main roadie. I wanted to — four months in Europe, great hotels, food, parties. But I was married and had young kids and … well, I digress.

Mack's new book appears to shine as brightly as a cluster of alien spacecraft in the night sky and almost as brightly as those Russian submarines I was tracking on sonar during my time in the Navy at Gitmo. I think you'll be fascinated by the depth of information in Mack's stories. Weird warships, NASA conspiracies, ghost stories, best places to see a UFO. I'm guessing you'll become a fan for life, just like I am of Keith Richards. You know, I worked a couple Stones' shows back in the day, and I actually got to touch one of Keith's guitars!

And just like that Stratocaster, you won't be able to put this book down!

A Message from Commander Cobra

Mack and I made contact/connection through my following his various opuses and his responding to a letter I wrote years ago. The bond of friendship made possible some demanding ops. This includes being a frequent wingman/co-host to the Wingman on his show "MMMXF" along with the eclectic Juan de Juan and other notable guests. "Mack Maloney's Haunted Universe" delivers unique source info and insight on various MMMXF stories, research for his varied fiction and nonfiction books, and television scripts. Any fan of the books and/or show will want this embedded intel on the full range of the Operation Distant Thunder mission.

—Commander Cobra sends/out.

Table of Contents

Ten Real Military X-Files

The Gallipoli Disappearance

On August 12, 1915, during the Battle of Gallipoli, a 100-man company of British soldiers known as the Sandringhams vanished into thin air.

They were last seen charging Turkish positions amid machine gunfire and bomb bursts. But when the smoke cleared, all of the soldiers had disappeared. A later search of the area turned up no evidence of what had happened. The soldiers' bodies were never found.

Even the British Army's then commander-in-chief couldn't explain the disappearance, saying later that "a very mysterious thing" had happened.

Two Years Early

On December 7, 1939, someone used white chalk to scrawl a message on the sidewalk outside a high school in Owensville, Illinois.

The message read: "Remember Pearl Harbor."

Exactly two years later, the Japanese launched their sneak attack on Pearl Harbor, bringing America into World War II.

The mysterious writer was never identified.

The Haunted Mud

One of World War I's fiercest battles took place near the village of Passchendaele, Belgium, from August to November 1917.

With a massive German army facing a similarly large force of British and Commonwealth troops across a no man's land, the battlefield had been hit with so much artillery that aerial photos later showed more than a million bomb craters in just a one-mile strip of land.

Due to heavy rains and thick mud (it had been the rainiest summer in 30 years), hundreds of soldiers on both sides vanished into the deep muck, never to be seen again.

Nearly a half-million men on both sides were killed or wounded in the battle. Almost 100,000 of the soldiers who died were never identified.

The D-Day Before D-Day

The Dieppe Raid, also known as Operation Jubilee, was a sort of trial run for the Normandy Invasion of World War II.

On August 19, 1942, a force made up primarily of Canadian soldiers landed in the French port city and battled the occupying German troops. It turned out to be an embarrassing loss for the Allies, though, with more than half the 6000-man force killed, wounded or captured. The rest had to be evacuated off the beaches.

Nine years later, in 1951, a husband and wife vacationing near Dieppe were awakened at 4 a.m. by the sounds of gunfire, shouting voices, and other noises of battle coming from the beach near their hotel.

For the next three hours, the couple meticulously documented everything they heard. Paranormal researchers later determined that their notes matched almost exactly what had happened during the Dieppe Raid.

The Rock Apes of Vietnam

As if being stuck in a senseless war halfway around the world wasn't enough, U.S. troops in Vietnam also had to endure attacks by Southeast Asia's own version of the Abominable Snowman.

They came to be known as the Rock Apes, and though the U.S. military never officially acknowledged them, these strange creatures were seen quite frequently by American soldiers during the war.

An interesting aspect about all the Rock Ape reports is that the description of the creatures was almost universal.

Red hair, muscular, bipedal, walking upright, some reaching six feet or more. And absolutely fearless.

Typical is the story told by Lieutenant Michael Kelley of the 101st Airborne Division. In 1969, he and his men were taking a break when eight of the strange creatures came casually walking up a trail in their direction.

The soldiers thought at first that they were Viet Cong and fired on them with machine guns and grenade launchers. In the midst of the firing, Kelley saw his men shooting at "ghostly images" that were swooshing through the bushes and trees all around them.

Throughout the frightening encounter, the ape-like beasts reportedly made sounds that sounded like dogs barking. Despite the gunfire, one ape rushed the soldiers snarling with teeth bared. Then, the creatures disappeared into the jungle. The soldiers later searched the area but found no bodies of the animals.

Three years earlier, in 1966, atop Hill 868 in Quang Nam Province, a battle was fought between Marines and a large group of Rock Apes. The Marines had reported that they'd detected a sizable force of Viet Cong headed their way. Their commander radioed his men to hold their fire and not give away their position. But then the Marines reported it was not the enemy after all — rather, dozens of Rock Apes had surrounded them.

The commander told his men not to open fire but to throw rocks at the creatures to scare them away. This was not a good idea, as the apes began throwing rocks back at the Marines, all the while screeching and growling. The Marines had to take cover to avoid the barrage of incoming missiles.

The creatures eventually retreated back into the jungle. The Marines later estimated that at one point, more than a hundred apes had surrounded them.

One of Our Submarines is Missing

On May 22, 1968, the American nuclear submarine *USS Scorpion* suddenly vanished.

After an extensive search, the Navy found the *Scorpion*'s wreckage two miles down at a point several hundred miles southwest of the Azores in the Atlantic Ocean. Its 99-man crew had perished.

The cause of the sinking has never been determined. Some believe the *Scorpion* launched a faulty torpedo that turned around and hit the sub. But others insist it was destroyed by the Soviet Navy after it was caught spying on top-secret Russian activities in the mid-Atlantic.

Pardon My Vomit

In 2007, the U.S. Navy awarded a contract to build a Puke Gun.

Technically called a "non-lethal stand-off weapon" and envisioned for use in hostage situations, the device could send radio frequencies through a wall and incapacitate anyone in the adjoining room by making them lose their balance, bringing on extreme motion sickness and severe projectile vomiting.

Little Bro Space Shuttle

Though the U.S. military does not deny its existence, it is tight-lipped about the X-37B spacecraft.

Looking almost exactly like the old space shuttle but a quarter the size, the unmanned craft launches from Vandenberg Air Force Base in California and can orbit for months without needing to return to Earth.

What's it doing up there? The Air Force will say only that it's "conducting experiments," but many believe the X-37B's real mission is one of two things: It's an extremely advanced spy craft — something that can easily be moved around in orbit to look down on trouble spots around the world — or it's a space-based nuclear bomber able to hit any target on Earth without interference from the people the nuke is going to land on.

A third possibility is the X-37B can do both.

Angels in Wartime, Part 1

On August 22, 1914, at the very start of World War I, the German Army was moving through Belgium, seeking to invade France. Blocking its way was the British Expeditionary Force.

The Germans had about 160,000 men, the British only half that many. The two armies clashed near Mons, a village in western Belgium, and after two days of fighting, the outnumbered British managed to stop the Germans, at least temporarily.

News of this "victory" swept through England, but with it came a bizarre account of how the British Army had received otherworldly assistance in the battle: It was said that just as the Germans were about to overwhelm the British, an army of ghostly archers appeared and fired at the enemy, slaying enough of them for the British to hold their ground.

The story's details vary after that, but the most popular version claimed the archers were actually angels appearing out of the sky to cut down the Huns and that many of the German soldiers killed that day had died of arrow wounds.

While several investigations after the war found little evidence that anything extraordinary occurred at Mons, the story of the heavenly warriors persists to this day.

Angels in Wartime, Part 2

A similar story about angels came out of another war on another continent.

Imperial Japan invaded China in 1931, marking the beginning of World War II. The Japanese Army brutalized the Chinese people for the next decade, including bombing many defenseless cities from the air.

A missionary named Dr. Charles Kimber was living in China at the time. In 1940, he received two letters on the same day. One was from a Japanese person he knew; the other from a friend who was Chinese.

The first letter described an incredible event. A Japanese pilot had been ordered to lead his bomber group against an undefended Chinese city. As the bomber formation approached its target, the lead pilot saw what he described as "a multitude of angels with drawn swords" blocking his way to the target.

(It might be interesting to note that Shintoism, which is the traditional religion of Japan, does not contain accounts of angels. It is more of a good spirit/bad spirit kind of faith.)

At first the pilot thought he was seeing an unusual cloud formation and continued leading his bombers onward. But as he drew closer, so many apparitions filled the sky that he was reluctant to go through them, so he turned around and headed back to base along with the rest of his formation. He was later executed for disobedience.

Now this is where it gets really weird. The second letter the missionary received that day described the exact same incident — the bombers, the angels, the dramatic retreat — but this time it was told, in great detail, from witnesses on the ground.

Top Places to See a UFO

1. Elk River, Minnesota

Aside from great fishing spots and beautiful snow-covered terrain, this small town north of Minneapolis had little more to offer … until the 1990s rolled around.

That's when residents began reporting strange things flying over their heads.

Witnesses said the UFOs appeared in a variety of forms, including ones shaped like cigars, wings, and very large V's. One object's size rivaled that of an airliner.

But the strangest report of all: one UFO spotted in 2008 looked like a huge jellyfish.

2. Bonnybridge, Scotland

This small town in the Scottish Midlands was known for its soaring development during the Industrial Revolution, its stunning landscapes, and as the home of '50s champion boxer Danny Malloy.

However, for the past two decades, people have recognized Bonnybridge for something else: multitudes of UFO sightings. It's the site of so many unexplained flying objects that the British government records at least one UFO report from the area every day.

In fact, since the mid-1990s, more UFOs have been reported around Bonnybridge than anywhere else on Earth.

3. Dubya's Ranch

The effects still linger from a series of spectacular UFO sightings in January 2008 over Stephenville, Texas, a small town just four minutes' flying time from former President George W. Bush's ranch in Crawford.

Witnesses described one object as being a mile-wide, extremely fast, and having intense bright lights. Some saw jet fighters pursuing this enormous craft; others claim the jets were actually escorting it. Radar reports confirmed something massive did fly through the central Texas skies around the time in question, and that the object was seen heading toward Bush's ranch.

If UFOs really are here to look for intelligent life, did these particular ETs know something we didn't?

4. Rachel, Nevada

There are three reasons why chances of seeing a UFO here are pretty good:

1. The main business in the tiny town (pop. 80) is called the "Little A'Le'Inn."

2. Rachel is located along a roadway the state of Nevada has officially christened "The Extraterrestrial Highway" (speed limit: "Warp 7").

3. Rachel is the closest town (just 27 miles away) to what many UFO enthusiasts consider their Shangri-La: the secret government air base at Groom Lake, aka Area 51.

5. <u>Dyfed, Wales</u>

The string of strange events that took place in and around Dyfed, Wales, in 1977 had a little bit of everything.

Residents reported seeing multiple UFOs, glowing balls of light chasing cars, alien beings walking about the countryside, some even looking in people's windows.

Other weird goings-on included a UFO that liked to hover over a schoolhouse; TVs, radios, and cars that stopped working for no reason; and even the teleportation of a large number of cattle from one place to another. Order your steak well done, Walter.

6. <u>Nullarbor Plain, Australia</u>

This place first made its bones as a UFO hotspot when the British military began testing atomic bombs there in the 1950s.

Since then, the extremely isolated area has become a center of intense UFO activity. People traveling through its harsh desert often experience sightings, including having their cars chased by UFOs.

As we'll learn later, this and many other incidents, including reports of alien abductions, forced the Australian government to erect a highway sign on entering the place that reads, "Beware of UFOs."

7. <u>Gulf Breeze, Florida</u>

This small city on the Florida Panhandle became famous in 1987 when a man named Ed Walters made public a number of dramatic photographs of UFOs.

Walters claimed the photos were the result of his own close encounters with ETs. Yet when researchers scrutinized the images, they declared them to be fakes.

But more than two hundred other witnesses have since come forward to report UFO sightings in Gulf Breeze, many backed up by photographs and videos depicting flying objects that look exactly like those that Walters had supposedly faked.

8. Chile's UFO Trail

Chile is famous for lots of things: eclectic music, fine wines, delectable cuisine … and numerous UFO sightings.

That's why the country's tourism board built the "UFO Trail," where adventurers may (or may not) get to see an ET or two. But only the hardiest should apply for this adventure.

One must first travel 150 miles south of the capital of Santiago to the small town of San Clemente. Then, it's a four-hour trip on horseback up into the Andes, climbing to a nosebleed altitude of nearly 10,000 feet. Only then does the 19-mile trek along the trail begin.

But should no UFOs show up, hikers will eventually find themselves on the *El Enladrillado,* a landscape consisting of 200 perfectly sliced granite-like blocks, thought to be a landing site for ancient astronauts.

9. Mount Adams, Washington State

Researchers consider this location a kind of Mecca when it comes to spotting UFOs because in many ways, the modern history of unidentified flying objects started right here.

On June 24, 1947, businessman Kenneth Arnold was piloting his private plane near Mount Adams when he spotted a line of nine strange-looking aircraft flying off his left wing.

By timing them as they flew between Mount Rainier and Mount Adams, Arnold was able to estimate the objects' speed at more than 1200 mph, a velocity unattainable by aircraft of the day.

Later describing their movements like "saucers skipping across the water," the term "flying saucer" was born. And apparently the saucers never left because locals say UFOs can still be seen flying around Mount Adams on an almost nightly basis.

10. Warminster, England

Located about 50 miles west of London, this quaint, cricket-loving town boasts a surplus of paranormal activity.

Starting in the 1960s, strange, unexplained sounds began rattling the residents. The racket was so frequent that citizens soon began referring to it as "The Thing." Then the UFOs arrived — and never left.

By one estimate, more than 5,000 unidentified flying objects have been spotted in the area over the years. As if that wasn't enough, in the 1980s, crops circles started popping up as well.

And to top it all off, just 15 miles away is Salisbury Plain, home of Stonehenge.

11. Earth Orbit and Beyond

They were seen during the Gemini orbital missions. They were seen on the way to the moon. Shuttle astronauts have spotted them; Russian cosmonauts have, too.

More than a dozen American and Russian space travelers have spoken openly about encountering UFOs during their missions, yet NASA doesn't want to talk about it.

What are they afraid of?

12. California

There's a secret UFO base near Catalina Island. UFOs are seen regularly -- from San Diego to San Francisco -- along the Pacific Coast Highway. An estimated one million people reported seeing a UFO dodging anti-aircraft shells over LA in February 1942.

Add in every sci-fi movie from "Earth vs Flying Saucers" to "E.T." to "Independence Day" and the fact that the Golden State always leads the country in unexplained sightings, there's only one conclusion: If you *really* want to see a UFO, California is the place to be.

Haunted USA

Fifty States … of Creepiness!

Alabama — The McCalla Hum

One day in late 2011, the residents of McCalla, Alabama, woke to hear a strange, unidentifiable noise.

No source could be found for the constant hum, described variously as "sirens in the distance," "locusts," or "the whirring of a helicopter," even though authorities thoroughly searched the town and the surrounding woods.

Residents speculate that past UFO sightings in the area might have had something to do with the bizarre noise.

Alaska — The Ghost Soldiers of Adak

Part of Alaska's Aleutian Islands chain, Adak Island was once a launching point for U.S. military attacks on Japanese forces occupying nearby islands during World War II.

Before the U.S. military left years ago, servicemen stationed on Adak reported seeing many strange apparitions.

In one chilling incident, a Marine on guard duty was shocked to see two lines of 1940s-era Japanese soldiers marching toward the island's so-called Toothpick Bridge. This was not just a glance or a brief hallucination. The Marine watched the ghost soldiers march all the way up to the bridge, something that took several minutes before they finally faded away.

Arizona — A Very Close Encounter

In the summer of 2009, four young people encountered a huge UFO and its occupants in the Arizona desert just west of Phoenix.

The witnesses described the UFO as being three-football fields-long and at least three stories high. Two of the witnesses approached the landed craft and were met by two somewhat humanoid occupants, one nine feet tall and the other about half that size.

The aliens told the witnesses that their mission was to prevent humans from destroying the Earth. They also warned that a "horrible event, from the Middle East, bigger than 9/11" would happen someday.

Their messages delivered, the craft took off, but the witnesses were later stopped by the military and questioned extensively about the strange event.

Arkansas — Mystery Quakes

Several years ago, the tiny community of Guy, Arkansas, experienced nearly five hundred earthquakes in just a few weeks' time, including fifteen quakes in one day.

Officials from the U.S. Geological Survey say the quakes happened right below the town.

While a local gravel company's operations were suspected at first, this theory was quickly discounted, leaving no explanation for the hundreds of quakes.

California — El Diablo's Nuclear Jellyfish

In April 2012, an unprecedented invasion of jellyfish-like sea creatures forced a nuclear reactor on the California coast to shut down.

A mysterious swarm of the gelatinous organisms, called salp, had so completely clogged screens used to filter the plant's cooling seawater that the utility company had to turn off its El Diablo reactor. Salps are usually found farther out to sea, so why the creatures chose to attack the plant's filtration system remains unknown.

Colorado — Flying Men of the SLV

It's believed that southeast Colorado's San Luis Valley experiences more paranormal activity than any other place in the United States. UFOs are routinely spotted there, along with ghosts, strange weather, "shadow people," Bigfoot-like monsters, and so-called prairie dragons, invisible, slug-like creatures that invade people's homes.

Strangest of all, though, have been the reports of flying humans. Said to be a cross between Dracula and the infamous Mothman, these flying men soar above the valley in full view of witnesses.

Nearly two dozen of the strange aerial creatures have been reported in the past few years, many by reliable people including policemen and local government employees.

Connecticut — Small State of Strangeness

Connecticut might be the third-smallest state, but it ranks near the top on America's weirdness scale. In recent years, the state has been besieged by hundreds of UFO reports, with one sighting described as "a cluster of alien ships floating overhead."

Dozens of encounters with unknown creatures also have been reported, including a mysterious animal hit and killed on one of the state's highways. Ghosts haunting homes and unexplained music have been reported from several towns as well.

Most bizarre are the reports from residents all over the state of horrific and terrible screams seemingly coming from nowhere.

Delaware — UFOs Haunt Racetrack

UFOs have long haunted the Dover Downs Racetrack in Dover, Delaware. Employees have been spotting mysterious objects over the racecourse for years, both day and night.

Described as bright spotlights that turn on and off, the UFOs arrive in groups of three to six and hover as if they are watching what's going on below.

Even more bizarre, any time the UFOs are seen, all cell phones in the area go dead.

Florida — The Haunted Launch Pad

Cape Canaveral's Launch Pad 34 is said to be haunted by the ghosts of three astronauts who died there after a tragic accident.

Spacemen Gus Grissom, Ed White, and Roger Chaffee were killed almost instantly on January 27, 1967, when a fire engulfed their Apollo I capsule as it was being tested for launch later that year.

Many witnesses, including NASA employees, say a weird feeling comes over anyone who approaches the now-abandoned launch pad, especially at night. More disturbing, sometimes the astronauts' dying screams can be heard.

Jurassic Georgia

In July 2008, two men on a hunting trip in northern Georgia heard an unusual rustling in the woods.

Seconds later, a lizard-like creature walked out of the bushes about a 100 yards in front of them. Both men later said the beast looked exactly like a Jurassic Park raptor — five feet tall, long tail, huge claws on both feet, with smaller claws on its short, stubby arms.

The hunters said the creature stopped for a moment, sniffed the air, and then disappeared back into the bushes.

Hawaii — The Night Marchers

Hawaii is full of strange things, none more so than the Hawaiian Night Marchers.

Numbering in the hundreds, these shadowy figures appear on deserted beaches long after dark, carrying blazing torches. They walk in formation, continuously moving forward, all night long, hence their name.

Witnesses are frequently made to feel uncomfortable when they see the ethereal displays, the result — Hawaiian legends say — of deceased family members warning their relatives to leave the ghosts in peace.

Idaho — The Mist at Sawyer's Pond

Just outside Emmett, Idaho, is a swimming hole called Sawyer's Pond.

One night in August 2012, a young couple drove out to the pond, but on arriving, said they felt something was not right. Walking to the water's edge, they were suddenly enveloped in a strange fog so dense they couldn't see.

When the boyfriend felt something squeeze his shoulder, the couple blindly ran back to their car. Once inside, the boyfriend confessed that he'd seen a human-shaped figure moving in the mist. The couple immediately fled the area.

While several people had reportedly drowned at the pond in recent years, there is still no explanation for what happened to the young couple that night.

Illinois— The Enfield Horror

On the evening of April 25, 1973, a young boy from Enfield, Illinois, was playing in his backyard when he was attacked by an extremely bizarre creature.

The boy described the monster as having three legs, a thick body, arms that came out of its chest, and two red eyes. The creature tore at the boy's feet before the youngster could get away.

A short time later, a neighbor saw the same creature and shot at it with a rifle, only to see it bound away at incredible speed. Other townspeople, including a TV newsman, had subsequent encounters with the beast.

A similar creature reportedly attacked people in a nearby town during the 1940s.

Indiana — The Elizaville Monster

An unusually large number of people have been reported missing from the tiny town of Elizaville, Indiana, over the past hundred years.

No one knows why, but current residents swear that a seven-foot-tall "man beast" has been spotted at night wandering the town's fields, lurking around its church, and especially haunting its cemetery.

Locals claim that if a person talks too loudly between the hours of 1 and 3 a.m., the monster will track them down, kill them, and then eat them, bones and all.

Iowa — Burlington's Flying Dragon

A number of Burlington, Iowa, residents have reported seeing a dragon flying over their city in recent years.

Two witnesses driving downtown late at night were the latest to spot the airborne creature. They described it as brown-skinned with an elongated, snake-like body and 15-foot long, bat-like wings. Its head was shaped like a seahorse, and a skinny tail flowed behind it.

Saying the dragon appeared to be slithering its way through the air, the witnesses watched the creature for several minutes until it finally disappeared into the night.

Kansas — Gateway to Hell?

The small town of Stull, Kansas, has a notorious reputation.

It is said that a small cemetery there, and a place halfway around the world in India, are the only two places on Earth where Satan appears in person.

Legend says the devil has been appearing in Stull since the 1850s and that the town's original name was

Skull. It was changed to cover its association with black magic.

Some visitors to the Stull Cemetery tell of being assaulted by a strong wind that holds them to the ground for some time, not allowing them to move. Still, every Halloween, witnesses show up at the tiny graveyard, hoping to catch a glimpse of Lucifer.

Kentucky — Return of the Goblins?

A Kentucky family has been regularly attacked by goblin-like creatures since 2011.

These beings stand about four feet tall, have large heads, large eyes, slits for mouths, and green skin. They frequently try to break into the family's home at night. The local police refuse to help the family, blaming wild animals for the problem.

In the fall of 1955, another rural Kentucky home was besieged by identical creatures. In what became known as the Hopkinsville Goblins Case, dozens of credible witnesses saw nightly attacks by the little green men before they abruptly stopped later that same year.

Louisiana — The Morgan City Monster

In December 2010, a nature photographer checked a trail camera he'd set up to film wild animals in a reserve in Morgan City, Louisiana.

He was shocked to find he'd caught the image of a ghostly humanoid figure instead. Advancing toward the lens, eyes wide and arms outstretched, the creature was all white and appeared somewhat transparent.

Though the camera had been smashed, its SIM card survived, preserving the image. Its owner, who chose to remain anonymous, made the photo available to a local TV station, which showed it continuously.

To date, no one has been able to explain the photo.

Maine — Real-Life Vampire Arrested

Police say a Maine man, charged with the murder of three Hell's Angels in 2011, was a real-life vampire. Arrested for executing three members of the notorious biker gang, the man claimed he drank the blood of one of his victims.

The defendant, who had undergone extensive surgeries to create devil-like horns on his forehead, had previously served time in prison after he and his 16-year-old girlfriend slashed a young girl's neck and then lapped up her blood.

While the suspect was known as Veiovis Caius (Veiovis being a Roman god of the underworld and Caius the name of a vampire from the Twilight series), his real name was Roy Gutfinski.

Maryland — The Beltsville Goatman

In 2000, construction workers near Bowie, Maryland, came face to face with a creature standing seven feet tall, weighing at least 300 pounds, and covered in fur.

The workers said the beast had the legs, hooves, and horns of a goat, but the upper body of a man. What the workers encountered was the Goatman, a monster that reportedly has been bedeviling nearby Beltsville, Maryland, for years.

While the creature is most often reported attacking cars with an ax, it's also been spotted throwing house pets off highway overpasses.

One story says the beast was once a scientist who, while working at the Beltsville Agricultural Research Center, conducted an experiment on goats that went horribly wrong.

Massachusetts — The Bridgewater Triangle

Located in southeast Massachusetts, the Bridgewater Triangle is a large swamp that's been the site of many UFO incidents, as well as reports of glowing orbs, flying balls of fire, Bigfoot appearances, and even sightings of giant snakes and monstrous dinosaur-like birds.

Add to this more than a dozen confirmed homicides that have taken place inside the triangle over the past 30 years. Almost a mini-version of Colorado's San Luis Valley, but with a somewhat bloodier past, Native American tribes reportedly cursed the swamp centuries ago after they'd received poor treatment from early colonial settlers.

Michigan — The Dogman

Sightings of a creature called the Dogman have been reported in Michigan since 1987.

In July of that year, an empty cabin near the small town of Luther was found to have deep claw marks around its door and windows, prompting local authorities to admit an "unknown animal" had tried to get in.

Ten years later, a witness camping in the forest near Luther heard a chilling howl, something more humanlike than a wolf or coyote. Later that night, the witness saw a creature across a narrow river bed, standing larger than a bear, with black fur, a long skull, and reflective yellow eyes.

The beast howled again, then ran up the bank and disappeared. Most startling, the creature ran not on all fours, but on two legs, like a human.

Minnesota — Ghost Train

In 2006, a group of friends in Elk River, Minnesota, went night fishing at a pond next to a long-abandoned railroad track.

Soon after arriving, the anglers were stunned to hear a train approaching. As the train sped by, the witnesses heard a blood-curdling scream and saw something fly off the last car, disappearing into some bushes. A disturbance then erupted from the bushes that was so violent it enveloped the fishermen in a wind that shook everything around them. The group quickly fled.

Coincidence or not, Elk River holds the distinction of being one of the top ten places in the United States to see a UFO.

Mississippi — Devil Worshiper's Road

There is one very creepy road in Waynesboro, Mississippi.

People claim that driving Shubuta Road virtually guarantees some extremely unsettling experiences. Engine failures are followed by cars shaking violently. Ghostly figures then appear and plant mysterious handprints all over the car's windows, as if they're trying to get in.

The locals believe occult sacrifices once took place along the road, leading to its haunting.

Missouri — The Black-Eyed Kid

One day, a Lawson, Missouri, housewife answered a knock at her front door to find a young girl she did not recognize.

The child was about seven years old, was wearing a dingy white dress, had dirty hair, and reeked of bad breath. She said she needed help and pleaded to come inside. But then the woman noticed that the strange girl's eyes were coal black, from rim to rim.

The woman immediately closed the door, locked it, and then locked every other door and window in her house. Traumatized by the experience, she sought medical attention and refused to leave her house for the next several days.

Dozens of reports of black-eyed children appearing at people's doors have surfaced from around the world in recent years.

Montana — The Timber Creek Monster

An unidentified creature has been wandering the hilly terrain around Timber Creek, Montana, for several years.

The creature has viciously attacked sheep herds in the area — in one month alone, it killed three-dozen ewes and seriously injured 70 more.

The beast's killing pattern is bizarre. While wolves and coyotes take only one or two sheep at a time, just enough to eat, the mystery beast seems to kill just for the thrill of it.

Local authorities are baffled that the creature's hunting habits are exactly like those of a hyena, a ferocious animal found only in Africa and Asia.

Nebraska — Cowboys and Aliens

On June 6, 1884, in a remote part of Nebraska, a group of cowboys rounding up cattle saw a fiery aerial object crash a few miles away.

Rushing to the crash site, the cowboys found the remains of a 50-foot-long cylindrical object glowing with intense heat. A local newspaper described the object as "an air vessel belonging to some other planet."

But four days later, the same newspaper reported a heavy storm had passed over the area and that rainwater had melted the craft's remains into a substance resembling salt.

Nevada — The Ghost of the Vegas Strip

Taxi drivers in Las Vegas swear this happens every Halloween.

Sometime around midnight, an unsuspecting cabbie will pick up a customer dressed like Elvis. The customer will ask to be taken to the Desert Inn, which was demolished years ago.

Thinking the customer is just another Halloween drunk, the cabbie drives him to The Wynn, where the Desert Inn once stood, but before arriving, the customer suddenly disappears.

The shocked driver stops to find the back of his cab empty except for a $20 casino chip always left behind on the seat.

New Hampshire — The Dover Jazz Ghost

A young woman newly relocated to Dover, New Hampshire, was at a jazz club late one night when she saw a man dressed in black and carrying a saxophone, staring at her from the shadows.

When the woman returned home, she saw the man again, sitting on a neighbor's lawn. Later that night, she heard sax music and, looking outside, saw the same man still on the neighbor's lawn, playing his sax.

When she called her neighbor the next morning to tell her what she'd seen, the neighbor was shocked. She said her brother was a musician and would often sit out on her lawn and play his sax — but he'd died tragically three years before.

New Jersey — The Mystery Shirts

On or about October 17, 1999, in a swamp located just off U.S. Route 70 in Brick, New Jersey, someone hung 17 men's dress shirts across a small patch of dead trees.

The shirts were all white, pressed and clean, and in pristine condition. Each one was hanging about twenty feet up, fastened to the tree with nails. Twelve days later, the number of shirts increased to 29, hung in the exact same manner.

No one has ever determined who placed the shirts there or why.

New Mexico — The Weeping Ghost

Colfax, New Mexico, was once a thriving Old West town. But when a young local boy suddenly died of an unknown illness in 1890, everything changed.

Beset with inconsolable grief, the boy's mother died a few months later, only to have her ghost return to haunt the local church.

Reports of her spirit sitting in the back row, sobbing uncontrollably, were so frequent that people started moving out of Colfax and eventually, the place became a real ghost town.

New York — Ghostly Whispers

Fort William Henry was built by the British in 1755 next to Lake George in upstate New York. It was the site of a massacre two years later during the French and Indian War, when French soldiers killed many of the fort's occupants and burned it to the ground.

A replica of the fort was built in the 1950s, and since then many visitors have captured shadowy figures in photographs and swear they hear voices whispering to them as they walk the grounds, urging them to leave.

The North Carolina Poop Monster

Something very creepy is living in the sewers of Raleigh, North Carolina.

Caught in a video that has since gone viral, the creature has been labeled the Poop Monster, because that's exactly what it looks like.

A spokesperson for the city's public utilities commission confirmed that "Poopy" appears to be a living creature, but offered no idea what it could be.

North Dakota — The Haunted Fort

Located in southwest North Dakota, Fort Abraham Lincoln is one of the most haunted places in the state.

Witnesses say they see a woman wearing a black dress pacing in front of the fort's barracks. They also hear the sound of children crying and the clamor of invisible horses stomping in the stables. Why is the place so ghostly? Maybe because it was from here, in June 1876, that George Custer and his 7th Cavalry left to do battle at Little Big Horn, never to return.

Ohio — The Thrice-Haunted Lake

An 11-foot tall, 1,000-pound ape-like monster known as Orange Eyes has been terrifying residents near Ohio's Charles Mill Lake since 1959.

The popular recreation site is also said to be the home of an armless, web-footed, green-eyed creature known as the Mill Lake Monster.

Even stranger, in October 1973, there was a bizarre encounter between a UFO and a military helicopter over the lake, leading many people to believe Orange Eyes and the Mill Lake Monster might be of extraterrestrial origin.

Oklahoma — The Oklahoma Octopus

A mysterious creature is said to inhabit Oklahoma's Lake Thunderbird.

Witnesses say the beast resembles an octopus, with long tentacles and leathery, brown skin. It kills unsuspecting swimmers by dragging them underwater and drowning them. This might account for the unusually large number of unexplained drownings in the lake since sightings of the monster first began.

While octopuses are normally saltwater creatures, certain species of jellyfish have adapted from saltwater to freshwater, and some cryptozoologists say the same adaptation is also possible for an octopus.

Oregon — The Mystery Rocks of Nehalem Bay

Nehalem Bay is located on the northern coast of Oregon. Legend says that when a gold-laden galleon was shipwrecked there, its crew buried their African slaves alive with the treasure, hoping their ghosts would keep the locals away.

These days, unusual piles of rocks mysteriously appear overnight near the rumored burial ground. Sometimes they consist of single piles; other times, of elaborate stacks.

No one has ever determined who's responsible for these strange displays.

Pennsylvania — When A Ghost Calls

One night in 2011, a paranormal investigator based in Danville, Pennsylvania, got a phone message from a man who wanted his home inspected for ghostly activity.

Identifying himself only as "George," the man left a phone number different from the one he was calling from.

The investigator called the number and asked the woman who answered if he could speak to George. After a long pause, the woman replied that George had been killed in a house fire ten years earlier.

When the investigator told her the number George had called from, the woman confirmed it was a number George had before he'd died.

Rhode Island — The Pawtucket Werewolf

On December 16, 2008, three boys playing hooky from school decided to explore some deep woods near Pawtucket, Rhode Island.

While walking along a stream bed, the boys saw a dark figure running through the brush nearby. The figure was humanoid in appearance, except its face was elongated like a wolf's.

The creature stopped and looked at the boys for a few moments, then disappeared into the woods. The truants later told police they were convinced they'd seen a werewolf.

South Carolina — The Gray Man of Pawley's Island

For the past hundred years, prior to hurricanes making landfall on South Carolina's Pawley's Island, a mysterious man appears on the beach and warns all who see him to leave the island.

There are numerous documented instances of witnesses encountering this strange man, dressed all in gray, as stormy weather is approaching.

Even stranger, residents who take the Gray Man's advice always find their homes undamaged after the storm. Those who don't invariably see their homes destroyed.

South Dakota — My Boss, the Ghost

Seth Bullock moved to Deadwood, South Dakota, in 1876 to build a hotel that still bears his name.

Though Bullock died in 1919, many guests have reported seeing his ghost in various parts of the inn.

Even stranger, the ghost seems to want to make sure the hotel staff works hard, because unexplained events always seem to occur whenever employees are goofing off.

Plates and glasses shake, lights turn themselves on and off, and items move on their own any time staff members find they have a few spare minutes on their hands.

Tennessee — The Tennessee Troll

One night in October 2008, a man driving to a relative's home in an isolated area of Tennessee nearly hit a dark figure sitting on the side of the road.

At first, the man thought it was a scarecrow. The figure was wearing a black hat and a shabby-looking black coat and had long, oddly shiny black hair. Its body was lumpy, as if stuffed with leaves.

But as he drove by, the figure turned and looked at him. It had glittering black eyes and a horrible, wrinkled, sunken-in face. The driver hit his gas and left the scene as quickly as possible. The man later did some research and concluded that he had seen a real-life troll.

Texas — The Ghost Light

The Texas Ghost Light can be found near Saratoga, Texas, on a dirt path called Bragg Road.

The light appears at random times at night, changing from yellow to white and swaying from side to side like someone waving a lantern. Some witnesses have attempted to approach the light with no success; others claim it has followed their vehicles while they drove on the darkened road.

Though local legend says the weird illumination is a lantern being carried by the ghost of a railroad worker killed in an accident nearby, exactly what causes the light remains a mystery.

Utah — Bulletproof Wolf

Soon after moving to a new ranch in central Utah, a family found an unusually large wolf sitting at their front door.

The strange animal acted as if it were their pet, but when it tried to snatch a farm animal, the rancher shot the creature six times at point-blank range. The bullets had no effect.

The wolf casually trotted across a field and disappeared. Since then, the ranch has been plagued by a musky odor and the constant buzz of ghostly voices, talking day and night.

Vermont — The Pigman

One night in 1971, a farmer who lived in Northfield, Vermont, heard strange noises coming from his backyard.

Expecting to find a raccoon going through his garbage, the farmer turned on an outside light to find a hideous creature hovering over his trash. Covered with white hair, the beast had the body of a man but the facial features of a pig.

After they stared at each other for a few seconds, the monster ran off into the woods. Dubbed the Pigman, it was seen by dozens of residents a few days later lurking outside a high school dance.

Since then, the Pigman has been spotted many times by motorists driving Northfield's country roads at night.

Virginia — Ghost of Bunnyman Bridge

Bunnyman Bridge is located on Colchester Road in Fairfax, Virginia.

Its name originates from a 1904 incident in which a patient escaped from a Fairfax insane asylum and survived for years in some nearby woods by eating uncooked rabbits. He eventually became known as the Bunnyman.

Every Halloween, the lunatic's ghost is said to emerge from the same woods, dressed as a rabbit, looking to murder unsuspecting trick-or-treaters with an ax.

Washington State — The Haunted Elevator

The Landmark Theater in Tacoma, Washington, is seriously haunted.

It began in 1929, shortly after the building opened, when a ghost was spotted in the audience during a performance. Since then, eerie shapes have frequently been seen in the theater's balcony.

Adding to the spirit count, one of the theater's janitors was accidentally killed in 1972, and his ghost has been riding the service elevator ever since.

Witnesses say the elevator goes up and down on its own and stops at random floors, where the doors open for several seconds, as if an unseen person is walking in or out.

West Virginia — The Bluefield Gargoyle

Is there a gargoyle living in Bluefield, West Virginia? One day in 2004, a boy in the small town was playing near a house owned by a reclusive family. The house had high hedges and was surrounded by barbed wire.

The boy heard a rustling in the hedges, and a moment later, a creature popped out. It looked like a huge, misshapen frog. It had sharp teeth, black eyes, green skin, long, pointed ears, and webbed feet that faced inward.

On seeing the boy, the beast opened its mouth, hissed, and then vanished back into the hedges.

Wisconsin — Strangeness at Bong Park

Visitors to the appropriately named Bong Park in southeast Wisconsin not only regularly see UFOs, but also report ghostly apparitions, strange fogs, mysterious noises, and unexplainable lights.

The park has a labyrinth of tunnels beneath it, left over from when the area housed a military airbase. But access to these tunnels is forbidden by federal law.

Wyoming — The Haunted High School

In 1940, a female student auditioning for a play at Natrona High School in Casper, Wyoming, was tragically killed. The school's auditorium has been haunted ever since.

Not only has the student's ghostly figure been seen on stage many times, but if someone sits in a certain front-row seat during a performance, something invariably goes wrong and the performance has to be stopped.

The girl's ghost has also been known to laugh hysterically during quiet moments of a show.

Mystery Sounds

Quackers

Starting in 1975, crews aboard Soviet submarines sailing in the North Atlantic began hearing strange noises in their headsets. The Russians called the high-pitched, frog-like sounds quackers.

At first the Soviets thought the noises were coming from a new kind of antisubmarine sound-detection system deployed by the U.S. Navy. But what would be the point of fielding sound detection technology that made noise?

The Russians subsequently discovered that some of the noises were being produced by objects traveling more than 125 mph underwater, a virtual impossibility.

The sounds are still heard today. Their source remains unknown.

The Bloop

Created in the 1960s, the U.S. Navy's Equatorial Pacific Ocean Autonomous Hydrophone Array is a system of underwater microphones capable of detecting sounds as soft as a burp at ranges of several hundred miles. In other words, it's the Navy's way of listening for hostile submarines operating in the Pacific.

But in 1997, the array recorded something totally unexpected: an extremely powerful underwater sound originating from a remote part of the Pacific off the southern tip of South America. The noise was so loud it was picked up on Navy undersea microphones more than 3000 miles away.

Dubbed the Bloop, it had no obvious origin other than it was not manmade. One scientist said that while the audio profile of the Bloop resembled that of a living creature, it was "far more powerful than the calls made by any animal on Earth."

Heard only that one time, the sound remains a mystery.

Mistpuffers

This sound has been described as distant but incredibly loud thunder heard even though skies are clear. Soldiers familiar with artillery say the noise is nearly identical to cannon fire.

Occasionally strong enough to cause shock waves that can rattle houses, Mistpuffers are reported all around the world, most often in waterfront communities. These include the banks of the river Ganges in India, the Finger

Lakes of New York State, the North Sea, and the coasts of Japan and Italy.

The mysterious sounds have been heard for hundreds of years. Early settlers in North America were told by the Iroquois Indians that the booms were the sound of the Great Spirit continuing his work of shaping the earth.

Their origin remains unexplained.

The Hum

The Hum is the common name for a series of phenomena involving a persistent humming noise heard by some people. Usually described as sounding like a diesel engine idling in the distance, the Hum has been reported in locations all over the world, most frequently in Taos, New Mexico, Bristol, England, and on the Big Island of Hawaii.

Not everyone hears the Hum. Some report it more frequently inside buildings; others feel vibrations throughout their bodies when hearing it. Using earplugs does not block out the sound and it is hard to detect with microphones. Its source and nature remain unknown.

Heavenly Horns

In January 2018, an unknown phenomenon known as the Trumpet Sound was heard literally all over the world.

The sound of a single trumpet blaring was reported by thousands of people in Spain, Switzerland, Indonesia, Malaysia, British Columbia, the U.K., New Orleans, and Los Angeles.

This same sound has been heard in the past but never to the degree of January 2018.

Explanations range from wind blowing through phone towers to the second coming of Christ, but the question remains: How could people from all around the globe be hearing the same sound?

Twelve Really Bad Military Ideas

1. Nuking the Moon

In the late 1950s, the U.S. Air Force decided America needed a boost in morale. With the launch of Sputnik, the first manmade object to orbit the Earth, Russia had taken a commanding lead in the space race. Something had to be done to switch the momentum back to America. So, the Air Force came up with a plan: Detonate a nuclear bomb on the moon, and do it at a time of day when Americans back on Earth could witness the event as it was happening.

Despite the fact the mushroom cloud and all its radioactive contaminants would have fouled the lunar landscape for eternity, the Air Force pushed the idea with the help of one of its biggest supporters, soon-to-be famous astronomer Carl Sagan. However, when the brass in Washington got together to discuss what was best for America they admitted that putting a man on the moon was a far better way to restore the nation's pride. In this rare case, the Pentagon actually got it right.

2. The Iceberg Aircraft Carrier

No less than Winston Churchill championed one of the strangest ideas of World War II: the iceberg aircraft carrier.

The notion surfaced in early 1942, when the Allies were facing a shortage of aircraft carriers to fight German U-boats in the Atlantic. Build a monstrous manmade iceberg, cover it with warplanes, and sail it (not sure how) into the Atlantic to do battle with the Nazi subs.

But even though scientists came up with a plausible way to construct the ship using a combination of sawdust and frozen water, one undeniable fact remained: Ice melts.

Plus, it was estimated that the price of building just one iceberg aircraft carrier would exceed the cost of an entire fleet of conventional carriers.

The fortunes of war turned in the Allies' favor before the idea got very far. It was finally given up for good in late 1943.

3. The Atomic Hand Grenade

Dreamed up in the 1950s, the idea was to build a nuclear bomb the size of a baseball to be used on the battlefield against masses of enemy armor. Such a weapon was to contain super-excited elements called isomers to generate the atomic blast.

However, the energy of just one isomer can equal the equivalent of 20 tons of explosives, which brings up the question: How could any soldier throw such a grenade and not get killed by his own blast?

4. America's Suicide Pilots

When the Cold War began, the United States had not yet developed an aircraft capable of carrying enough fuel to drop a nuclear bomb on Russia and return home safely. So the Pentagon took a page right out of Japan's war tactics manual and proposed sending American pilots on one-way kamikaze missions to Russia.

Thankfully, in the early 1950s, jet-powered bombers like the B-36 and B-47 were introduced. These aircraft could fly to Russia, drop a nuke, stay out of the way of the blast (a bonus), and make it home safely with fuel to spare.

5. The Flying Dorito

In 1983, U.S. defense contractors McDonnell Douglas and General Dynamics teamed up to win a Navy contract to design an all-weather, carrier-launched stealth aircraft called the A-12 Avenger II.

But when the project was completed, what the Navy got instead was a plane with a cool nickname ("The Flying Dorito" for its triangular shape) but also a multitude of flaws, cost overruns, and a history of colossal mismanagement.

The A-12 never got off the drawing board and was canceled in 1991. The cost to taxpayers for a plane that never flew: $5 billion.

6. Because Salmon Swim Upstream

It was a dream scenario back in the 1950s: design a plane that was half helicopter, half combat fighter to fulfill the Navy's desire to have all its vessels — not just aircraft carriers — carry warplanes.

Designated the XFV "Salmon," with its landing gear located in the tail, it could take off vertically then turn over to level in mid-flight and fly normally. The revolutionary design would have been perfect except for one significant flaw: It was just about impossible for the plane to reverse the process and land, simply because the pilot could not see behind him.

7. The Nuclear-Powered Nuclear Bomber

The idea here was to design an aircraft that could harness the power of an onboard nuclear reactor and stay in the air for several weeks without needing to land or refuel. Basically a flying battleship, there would be three rotating crews, quarters to house them, a dining hall, lavatories, the works.

But there were problems.

First, the more time such a plane was airborne, the more time the crew would be exposed to its reactor's deadly radiation. It was estimated that *twelve tons* of lead would be required just to protect the crew — virtually impossible from an aerodynamics point of view. Second, the plane would have been so enormous it would have required a hangar the size of football field to house it and a runway three miles long for takeoffs and landings. Then there was the threat of the plane crashing while carrying all of that nuclear material.

Seeing very little upside, the Pentagon scrapped the idea in 1961.

8. The Intruder from the Future

Built to fly 15 miles high at three times the speed of sound, the B-70 "Valkyrie" nuclear-armed bomber had the potential of being the greatest weapon ever made. Nicknamed "The Intruder from the Future," it was a huge aircraft with a fantastic swept-wing shape right out of a 1950s science fiction movie.

The Valkyrie was intended to go so fast it would basically ride above its own shock wave, just like a surfer rides atop an ocean wave. However, the plane's architects soon discovered major flaws in their initial design, causing numerous delays and massive cost overruns.

By the time the first Valkyrie flew in 1964, it was already deemed obsolete.

9. Holy Batbomb!

Desperate to attack Japan early in World War II, the U.S. military came up with a truly batty idea: Attach tiny time bombs to live bats, then release millions of them over Japan. The bats would hide in buildings and homes until their bombs went off, causing widespread fires.

Though FDR himself approved the idea, the Army abandoned it after a swarm of the armed bats was released by accident and burned down an air base in New Mexico.

10. The Other Pussy Galore

Back in the 1960s, the CIA spent $20 million trying to turn a cat into a spy.

With a microphone embedded in its ear and an antenna taped along its back, the plan was to let the animal loose near the Soviet embassy in Washington, where it would hopefully encounter some Russians and pick up conversations containing useful intelligence.

But the idea went wrong on its very first try when, just seconds after being released by its CIA handlers, the $20 million spy cat was run over by a taxi.

11. How High Can You Fly?

In 1915, in the midst of World War I, the British government asked the Royal Air Force to design an armored car. Just why the air corps was expected to create a piece of land armor is unclear, but the RAF plunged right in and created the Sizaire-Berwick Armored Car.

It had everything called for in the specifications including armor and machine guns. But instead of a typical engine, the RAF fitted it with a propeller in the rear, thinking this would be a good way to propel it across the battlefield.

They were wrong. Not only did this prop-driven design barely get the armored car moving, the aircraft engine and the propeller itself were not protected in any way. One enemy bullet in the right place would disable the Wind Wagon permanently.

Luckily for the people who would've had to ride in it, the RAF invention was quickly rejected.

12. The Doomsday Bomb

It was a rumor that circulated during the Cold War: If the Russians ever found themselves losing a nuclear exchange, they planned to explode a bomb that would end all life on Earth.

Said to be constructed of cobalt, once detonated, this weapon would have blanketed the planet with a cloud of ultra-long-lasting radioactive fallout, meaning that even people who'd made it into shelters wouldn't be able to emerge for many, many years, if ever.

Worst Spies Ever

Exotic, alluring — and dumb

Margaretha Geertruida Zelle, aka Mata Hari, was an unemployed Dutch dancer who reinvented herself as the world's most famous stripper, prostitute — and spy.

She serviced many Allied military officials during World War I, pumping them for information during copulation and then selling the intelligence to Germany. Eventually arrested by the French, she denied knowing anything about espionage — but then made the mistake of offering to spy for France *against* Germany.

But why, her captors asked her, would a person with no knowledge of espionage offer to become a spy? Mata Hari had no good answer. She was executed by a firing squad soon afterward.

Communist Party Animal

During the mid-1950s, Russia's top KGB agent, Rudolph Abel, built a spy network in the United States so large, and so successful, that Moscow was forced to send him an assistant.

Named Reino Hayhanen, he was a senior KGB operative highly trained in the art of espionage. But once he landed in New York City, Hayhanen began a campaign of alcohol abuse, gambling, and whore-mongering that was relentless. His idea of a good time was to become intoxicated in the company of prostitutes and then tell them some of the world's most sensitive secrets.

On learning of this behavior, Moscow ordered Hayhanen back to Russia for punishment. Instead, the wayward spy stole $5,000 in KGB money, fled to Paris, nearly drank himself to death, and then surrendered to the U.S. Embassy. Within weeks, the powerful Soviet spy ring was smashed and Rudolph Abel was in prison.

Hayhanen would later die in a car crash on the Pennsylvania Turnpike that some researchers have deemed mysterious.

The Gang That Couldn't Spy Straight

In the 1990s, eleven Russian espionage agents set new levels of incompetence when it came to the business of spying.

Sent to the U.S. on a "deep-penetration" mission, one member of the gang turned her laptop over to an undercover FBI agent so he could fix it. She later registered a new cell phone, listing her address on the application as "99 Fake Street."

Two other ring members sent notes to their commanders in the Kremlin complaining about Moscow's refusal to buy them a swanky house in New Jersey. Others basically forgot all about their mission and partied like it was 1999.

When they were finally caught, the gang had accomplished so little that the U.S. could only charge them with being unregistered foreign agents before booting them out of the country.

The Big Mouth

Stewart David Nozette, once a distinguished NASA scientist and defense analyst with a top-secret clearance, was arrested by the FBI in 2009 in part for telling people that he'd like to be a spy.

While investigating him for falsifying government expense reports, the FBI uncovered an email in which Nozette stated he would gladly spy for a foreign country — if the price was right. When FBI agents posing as Israeli intelligence agents reached out to Nozette, he all but asked them: "What took you so long?"

After handing over classified information to these undercover agents, Nozette was arrested and charged with spying for Israel, even though the Israelis had never recruited him.

The Beirut Pizza Hut Spy Ring

Was it the free breadsticks? The cheap chicken wings on Wednesdays? Or the additional topping for only a dollar?

Whatever the reason, a major U.S. spy ring was busted in Beirut in 2011 after the people it was supposed to be spying on, the terrorist organization Hezbollah, discovered that the ring was lunching regularly with its CIA employers at a Beirut Pizza Hut. In fact, whenever the CIA wanted to meet its paid informants, it would always send them the same code word: "PIZZA."

Asked why Pizza Hut was the CIA's eatery of choice, an agency spokesperson sniffed, "We do not discuss operational activities."

A Woman Scorned

U.S. Navy specialist John Walker spied for the Soviet Union from 1968 to 1986, selling classified information to Moscow in return for $1 million. But instead lying low to conceal his treason, Walker embarked on a conspicuously lavish lifestyle, including buying not one, but two expensive sailboats.

Things began to unravel when Walker's ex-wife, who knew about his spying, demanded he pay her more alimony. When Walker refused, she contacted the FBI and told them everything. Walker was arrested, convicted, and sentenced to life in prison.

Putting on the Ritz

In 1997, the Mossad, Israel's intelligence agency, decided to recruit a spy inside the famed *Hotel Ritz* in Paris. Notorious Middle Eastern arms dealers were known to stay there when in France, so an operative working on the inside might result in an intelligence bonanza.

To this end, Israeli agents approached the Ritz's head of security, Henri Paul. Despite an ongoing battle with alcohol, Paul had access to the entire hotel and could eavesdrop on the VIP guests he frequently chauffeured around town.

But Paul's spy career was short-lived. Just days after agreeing to work for Israel, he was asked to drive two VIPs from the hotel to a nearby apartment building. The VIPs were Princess Diana and her boyfriend Dodi Fayed, and it was Paul — drunk at the wheel — who crashed their car in a Paris underpass, killing them both and himself.

"Look at Me, I'm a Spy!"

Karl Lody, a reserve officer of the Imperial German Navy, was quite possibly the worst spy of World War I.

Approached by German Intelligence in 1914 to gather information on British military installations, Lody obliged and was soon in the U.K.

But he was sloppy from the start. He aroused suspicions by showing up at the British naval base at Rosyth, Scotland, and asking pointed questions about the warships anchored there. He subsequently traveled to London and made an appearance at a British anti-aircraft installation, bluntly asking how many guns it took to shoot down a German zeppelin.

Lody was put under surveillance after a series of letters he'd written to his German controllers were intercepted by British authorities. Unaware his cover was blown, he traveled to Liverpool, where he was seen drawing sketches of warships in the harbor.

He was arrested soon afterward, and though he gained some sympathy from his British jailers, he was eventually executed in the Tower of London.

Double-Crossing the Twisted Cross

In what would seem to be the most successful intelligence triumph of all time, Britain's security service MI-5 caught *every* Nazi spy sent to the U.K. during World War II. What's more, the British convinced all of these captives to broadcast disinformation back to their German masters, totally fouling the Nazis' espionage effort.

In truth, though, the Nazis were fantastically stupid in selecting spies, as most of the German agents simply turned themselves in to authorities upon reaching British shores.

Clever ... except once

Disgraced CIA employee Aldrich Ames was one of the most damaging spies in U.S. history.

Between 1985 and 1994, he sold secrets to the Russians in return for millions of dollars. Clever and arrogant, Ames was also good at covering his tracks. Even when he knew his CIA bosses suspected him, he continued feeding intelligence to Moscow, almost daring his employers to catch him.

They finally did — because of one mistake. In October of 1992, Ames routinely told his bosses he was traveling to Columbia to visit his wife's family. Actually, he flew to Venezuela and met with a Russian agent. The FBI was there, watching him. Ames was eventually arrested, convicted and sent to prison for life.

The Case of the Purple-Pissing Japanese

One can find success as a spy, creating a lifestyle rivaling the rich and famous. But as is the case for some, one lapse in judgment and it all comes crashing down.

FBI agent Robert Hanssen spied for the Russians from 1979 to 2001, earning $1.4 million in blood money. Like Aldridge Ames, Hanssen was good at covering his tracks. But also like Ames, one misstep did him in.

Knowing it had a traitor in its midst, the FBI purchased a tape recording from an ex-Soviet agent on which the unnamed mole was heard mentioning the "purple-pissing Japanese," a peculiar phrase originally attributed to General George Patton. One FBI analyst listening in realized he'd heard an FBI agent say those odd words before.

That agent was Robert Hanssen. Arrested for multiple acts of espionage, Hanssen was convicted and sentenced to life.

The Drooling Idiot

Imagine someone who never wore a clean shirt, dressed in rolled-up, wrinkled suits, spoke in indecipherable mumbles, and drooled so much his telephone had to be sanitized daily.

Now imagine this person running the CIA.

His name was William Casey, and he was America's top spy from 1981 to 1987. Casey was at the heart of many disastrous CIA programs, including the 1981 Iran-Contra scandal, in which he illegally approved selling weapons to Iran in exchange for hostages — the same Iranians who, one year later, blew up a military barracks in Lebanon, killing 241 U.S. Marines.

For Whom the Spy Tolls

In between watching bullfights, shooting wild game and drinking heavily, premier American writer Ernest Hemingway somehow found time to be a Russian spy.

Or at least he tried to be. According to the book, "Spies: The Rise and Fall of the KGB in America," Hemingway met with Soviet agents in the early 1940s and expressed a willingness to help the Russian cause. Once recruited, he was given the code name Argo.

But apparently Papa was not as good a spy as he was a writer. He failed to give Moscow any valuable information, and contact between Hemingway and the KGB ended sometime around 1950.

Staunch Patriot, Lousy Spy

Nathan Hale, the Revolutionary War hero famous for declaring, "I regret that I have but one life to lose for my country" before the British hanged him for espionage, was actually a terrible spy.

Sent to New York City to determine British troop levels, Hale was befriended by a man named Robert Rogers. When Rogers confided to Hale that he, too, was an American spy, Hale told him everything about his own secret mission— and was promptly arrested and executed.

Rogers *was* a spy — for the British. Said one historian about Hale's misadventure: "How could anyone on a secret mission be so stupid as to disclose the object of his mission to a perfect stranger?"

Despite Hale's failure as a secret agent, a life-size statue of him occupies a place of honor at CIA headquarters in McLean, Virginia.

Spooky Action at a Distance

Just Watch Me

There's a quantum mechanics experiment that's baffled scientists for decades. It's called the Double-Slit experiment, and the idea is to determine if light is a wave or made up of particles.

It can be challenging to put into words, but here goes.

On one side of a box, a scientist attaches a laser with the ability to shoot photons, the building blocks of light. The other end of the box is just a plain wall.

In between, the scientist puts a piece of cardboard with two vertical slits.

The scientist shoots photons through the slits to see what kind of pattern they'll create on the wall on the other side of the box. In theory, if light is made up of particles, the photons will make two stripes on the wall that are simply mirror images of the two slits. But if light is a wave, there will be a pattern of many stripes on the wall, like a series of ocean waves interfering with each other before hitting a dock.

Whenever this experiment is carried out, if the scientist observes the experiment, watching which slits the photons go through, the photons will make the two stripes on the wall, indicating light is made up of particles.

However, if the scientist *does not* watch the experiment — if it takes place within a closed environment — the photons will make the pattern of many stripes, meaning that they are acting like waves.

In other words, the result of the experiment depends on whether someone is watching or not.

Scientists cannot explain why this happens.

Untangling the Entanglement

It was Albert Einstein himself who coined the term "Spooky Action at a Distance," and he did not use the word "spooky" lightly.

Pretend electrons are like marbles. You take two marbles, flick them with your fingers at the same time, and get both spinning in the same direction. Now, you flick just one marble with your finger and get it spinning in the opposite direction. No big deal.

But if the marbles were positively charged electrons, the second electron would start spinning in the opposite direction, too, whether it was right next to its partner — or at the opposite end of the universe. No matter what the distance separating them, what you do to one electron will affect the other electron as well.

It's called entanglement, and like the Double-Slit Experiment, no one knows why it happens.

No Fred or Wilma, but ...

When we look up at the stars at night, in just about every case, the light we see has been traveling toward us for millions of years. In effect, looking out into space is looking back in time.

So suppose you were able to jump in a rocket ship that could go faster than the speed of light and travel to a planet a hundred million lightyears away. Once there, if you had a telescope powerful enough to look back to Earth, you would see the dinosaurs roaming our planet.

But Could You Dunk It?

Atoms are largely empty space. If all the empty space between all the atoms in the universe were removed and everything was pushed together as closely as possible, the result would be about the size of a basketball.

Is That Sand in Your Shoes?

According to researchers at the University of Hawaii, there are seven quintillion, five hundred quadrillion grains of sand on Earth. Yet, according to the latest estimates, there are 100 billion trillion stars in the universe. This means not only are there more stars than grains of sand on Earth, there are actually *multiple* stars for every grain.

Soap Opera

Einstein's hair was always a mess because he used ordinary bar soap to wash it. When someone asked him why he didn't use soap on his body and shampoo for his hair, he replied: "Two soaps? Too complicated."

The Unexplainable

The Meowing Nuns

In the 1844 book *Epidemics of the Middle Ages*, J. F. C. Hecker gave an account of a nun in a convent in France who began to meow like a cat. She didn't know why she was doing it, but she couldn't stop.

Soon, other nuns began meowing, too. In days, the whole convent was afflicted.

This disrupted people in the surrounding neighborhoods and soldiers were finally called in to fix the situation. Their tactics were extreme but direct. The soldiers beat the nuns until the holy women promised to stop meowing.

During this era in France, cats were thought to be in league with the devil.

Tunguska

On June 30, 1908, an explosion ripped through the air above a remote forest in Siberia, near the Tunguska River.

The fireball was at least seventy miles wide, burning up nearly one hundred square miles of forest and leveling more than eighty million trees. While there were no reports of human casualties, hundreds of charred reindeer carcasses were later found at the site.

Whatever caused the explosion, it is still one of the most powerful blasts ever recorded — one hundred eighty-five times more powerful than the Hiroshima atomic bomb. It was picked up on seismometers as far away as England.

The Tunguska region of Siberia is a very isolated place. It has a short summer and a long winter, and is extremely hard to get to. When the explosion happened, nobody ventured to the site to investigate because Russia was embroiled in political strife at the time.

It was not until 1927 that a team of Russian scientists finally made a trip to the area. Incredibly the damage was still apparent, almost twenty years later.

They found a large area of flattened trees spreading out more than thirty miles. There was no impact crater or any kind of space-borne debris, belying the theory that a meteor hit the Earth.

Some Russian scientists later theorized that a comet was to blame, as comets are made up mostly of ice and would leave little solid debris. Other researchers suggested it could have been caused by matter and antimatter colliding over Siberia, but they could never explain under what circumstances that would have happened. Still others believe a nuclear explosion somehow caused the blast, or that an alien spaceship crashed at the site.

But the exact reason of the Tunguska explosion has never been found.

Miracle ... or the Largest UFO Sighting Ever?

In the spring and summer of 1916, three children from a small rural village about 60 miles north of Lisbon, Portugal, claimed to have been visited by an angel.

This heavenly body appeared to them three times just outside the village of Fatima, telling them he was the guardian angel of Portugal. He urged them to pray for peace and prepare themselves for an even more fantastic vision sometime in the future.

About a year later, on May 13, 1917, the same three children were tending sheep in a small grove near their village when they claimed they saw a vision of the Virgin Mary. This apparition also urged them to pray for peace and an end to all war, promising to appear to them on the thirteenth of every month for the next six months.

Though the children had agreed among themselves to keep the incident a secret, word soon leaked out. A month later, on June 13, about seventy people were in attendance in the small grove — but only the three children claimed to see the apparition. The number of spectators tripled for the July visit, during which the apparition gave the three children a gloomy prediction of a world endlessly wracked with war and suffering.

The August visit was delayed a bit when a local civil administrator, part of Portugal's solidly anti-religious government, had the three children put in jail. Threats to the children to recant didn't work, though. They stood by their story, which only served to spread word of their visions even further.

Though the August visit took place six days later than prophesized and only in front of the children, on September 13, 30,000 people were on hand in the grove. As historians point out, this was an enormous crowd for rural Portugal.

But it was nothing compared to the October 13 vision. On that morning, *70,000* people were on hand — and many of them saw a truly amazing sight.

That day dawned cloudy and rainy, but just before the time the apparition was expected, the precipitation suddenly stopped. Most of the clouds parted, leaving only a thin layer to cover the sun, just enough so it could be seen without hurting the eyes.

When one of the children urged those gathered to look skyward, thousands in the crowd saw the sun begin to rotate and change colors. Many others saw it almost fall to the Earth, coming so close it dried their rain-soaked clothes. Others saw it zigzagging. Some reports say the sun's bizarre movements were seen by people up to forty miles away.

A number of newspaper reporters were in the crowd and they swore that these things happened.

One of these journalists was Avellino de Almeida, a reporter for Portugal's most influential newspaper, *O Seculo*. The newspaper was pro-government, meaning it was staunchly anti-religious. Still, Almeida reported the following: "Before the astonished eyes of the crowd, whose aspect was biblical as they stood bare-headed, eagerly searching the sky, the sun trembled, made sudden incredible movements outside all cosmic laws. The sun 'danced' according to the typical expression of the people."

A physician named Dr. Domingos Pinto Coelho was also on hand. Writing for the newspaper <u>Ordem</u>, he reported, "The sun, at one moment surrounded with scarlet flame, at another aureoled in yellow and deep purple, seemed to be in an exceeding fast and whirling movement, at times appearing to be loosened from the sky and to be approaching the earth, strongly radiating heat."

A third reporter, representing the Lisbon newspaper *O Dia*, wrote: "The silver sun, enveloped in the same gauzy purple light, was seen to whirl and turn in the circle of broken clouds … The light turned a beautiful blue, as if it had come through the stained-glass windows of a cathedral, and spread itself over the people who knelt with outstretched hands. People wept and prayed with uncovered heads in the presence of a miracle they had awaited. The seconds seemed like hours, so vivid were they."

So what really happened at Fatima?

As many ufologists have suggested, the answer may lie in subtracting the element of religion from the episode. Though the Portuguese government was virulently antireligious, the country's population itself was overwhelmingly Catholic. Had these events happened in a place that was decidedly more secular, with a citizenry more diverse in its religious beliefs, the story might read differently.

Another worldly visitor contacts three children, telling them to prepare for another even more important cosmic visitor. This second visitor appears to them, as promised, on the same day of the month, for a half a year. On the sixth and final visit, a massive crowd of witnesses sees a colorful silver disk dancing across the sky, giving off sparks, coming so close to them its heat can dry their clothes.

With a few tweaks, this description sounds not unlike many UFO reports — leading some to claim that the whole episode was actually a massive "close encounter" with a UFO.

Most interesting, UFOs are still reported frequently around Fatima today.

Hitler's BFF's Mystery Mission

If such a thing were even possible, Rudolph Hess was Adolf Hitler's best friend.

He edited Hitler's autobiography, *Mein Kampf*, and in 1939 was recognized by the Fuehrer as third in line of succession for the Nazi Party.

Hess was known for his absolute loyalty to Hitler and was frequently referred to as the Fuehrer's right-hand man. This made the events of May 10, 1941, all the more baffling.

Unbeknown to a lot of people, Hess had learned how to fly. On the night of May 10, he requisitioned an Me-110 night-fighter from a Luftwaffe airbase in Augsburg and flew … to Scotland. Once over Eaglesham, a village just south of Glasgow, Hess bailed out and was captured by local farmers.

Why did he do it?

No one is really sure. The most accepted explanation is that Hess wanted to broker a peace agreement between England and Germany, but if so, he'd planned it without first checking with his bud, Adolf. Furious at Hess's action, Hitler condemned his friend, calling him a madman suffering from "pacifist delusions."

Hess was held in England as a POW for the rest of the war and later locked up in Berlin's Spandau Prison. He was found hanged there on August 17, 1987. Though there was evidence that his death was a suicide, conspiracy theorists insist he was murdered by MI6, Britain's intelligence service.

Atomically Unlucky?

On August 6, 1945, the United States dropped the first atomic bomb on Japan, obliterating the city of Hiroshima.

At the time, Tsutomu Yamaguchi, a 29-year-old naval engineer, was on a three-month-long business trip to Hiroshima for his employer, Mitsubishi Heavy Industries. August 6, 1945 was his last day in the city and he was looking forward to returning home to his wife and infant son.

Yamaguchi was horribly burned in the Hiroshima blast, but managed to get out of the devastated city and head for home. Unfortunately, his home was in Nagasaki.

He arrived there on August 9, just in time to get caught up in the blast of America's second A-bomb drop, and was badly burned once again.

In 2009, the Japanese Government officially recognized Yamaguchi as being the only person present at both atomic blasts.

He died in 2010 at the age of 93.

The Phantom Tunnels of Shinjuku Station

Japan's Shinjuku Station is the busiest subway station in the world.

Located in the middle of Tokyo, it boasts thirty-six platforms, twenty different tracks, twelve different rail lines, 200 entrances and exits, and countless subterranean levels. Nearly *four million* commuters use it on a typical day.

But…Shinjuku has another name: the Bermuda Triangle of Tokyo. The place is so huge and so elaborate, that some Tokyo residents insist there have been instances of commuters going into the station, never to be seen again.

Wrong turns, wrong stairs, wrong elevator, the doomed are said to finally find themselves in an empty hallway, deep underground, with no way out.

The Ghost Blimp

The blimp was known as Love-8.

It was attached to the U.S. Navy's Airship Patrol Squadron 32 based on Treasure Island in San Francisco Bay. About 150 feet long and 47 feet in diameter, it could fly at just under 40 miles an hour.

On August 16, 1942, Love-8 was assigned to early patrol duty, looking for Japanese submarines within a 50-mile radius of San Francisco. The patrol would take about four hours, and Love-8 was expected to return to base no later than 10:30 that morning.

The blimp took off from Treasure Island at 6 a.m. with a two-man crew: Lieutenant Ernest Cody and Ensign Charles Adams. Cody was at the controls. The day was overcast, but the visibility was good.

Ninety minutes later, Cody radioed the blimp's position as near of the Farallon Islands, about 30 miles west of San Francisco. Four minutes after that, Cody sent a second message: "Am investigating suspicious oil slick — stand by."

Because an oil slick might indicate an enemy sub, the blimp dropped two smoke flares and began searching the area.

The Liberty ship *Albert Gallatin* was nearby, as was a fishing boat. Their crews saw Love-8 dropping the smoke flares and watched as the airship circled the scene for nearly an hour. At one point, the blimp got so close to the fishing boat the fishermen could clearly see two men inside.

But that would be the last time Cody and Adams were ever seen again.

Shortly after 9 a.m., the crew of the fishing boat saw Love-8 climb and turn back toward San Francisco. The blimp's last radio message was the one sent at 7:34, informing their base that they were circling the oil slick. Now the base was repeatedly calling Love-8 but getting no response. Two search planes were sent out to look for the blimp.

Two hours later, around 11 a.m., a Pan Am airline pilot spotted Love-8 passing over the Golden Gate Bridge. Shortly afterward, one of the search planes saw the blimp about three miles off the coast, flying east. An Army P-38 pilot also spotted the blimp around this time. All three pilots reported nothing unusual and assumed Love-8 was headed back to Treasure Island.

At approximately 11:15 a.m., more than five hours after it left Treasure Island, the blimp was seen approaching Ocean Beach in San Francisco. It touched down briefly on the beach and then moved inland. Fifteen minutes later it descended toward Daly City, a suburb south of the San Francisco county line. It came to rest in the middle of the 400 block of Bellevue Avenue, its gas bag nearly deflated.

An off-duty firefighter rushed to rescue Love-8's crew, but when he looked inside the blimp's gondola, nobody was in the cabin. More firefighters arrived, and they began tearing into the blimp's envelope, certain the two men were trapped inside. But they found no sign of Cody or Adams.

The Navy immediately launched a search for the missing men. For the next three days, air raid wardens and highway patrolmen scoured the area around Ocean Beach where L-8 had drifted ashore. Meanwhile, Navy ships and planes assisted by the Coast Guard searched the waters off San Francisco.

But it was all for naught. Cody and Adams were never found.

So what happened to the Love-8 between the time its crew spotted the oil slick and when it came to rest on Bellevue Avenue?

There were many theories. The crew was somehow captured by a Japanese sub. Or they were spying for Japan and rendezvoused with a U-boat to escape. Maybe a stowaway had overpowered the two men and then somehow vanished as well. Possibly their disappearance was actually an AWOL scheme, or that one crewman murdered the other over a woman, dumped his body, then fell overboard himself. Or perhaps a rogue wave hit Love-8 after it temporarily dipped into the ocean, washing away both men. The perennial favorite, of course, is that Cody and Adams were abducted by aliens.

But just how two naval officers vanished from one of the most heavily trafficked areas around San Francisco while their blimp was being tracked by ships and planes, not to mention people on the ground, remains a mystery.

The Navy closed the book on the incident a year later, officially classifying it as "one hundred percent unknown."

When UFOs are Not Flying Saucers

The Scare Ships

It all started one early morning in 1909, when a policeman in Peterborough, England, saw a strange, massive object go over his head.

It was flying at about 1,000 feet, was oblong and narrow, and had powerful searchlights attached to its underside. It was so large -- later estimated at 300-feet or more -- it blotted out the stars. And it was moving at tremendous speed. As the policeman watched in astonishment, it vanished to the northwest.

Within six weeks there were hundreds of similar sightings all over England. So many people claimed to have seen the same huge, cigar-shaped object it was soon clear there was more than one. Thus, the media dubbed them the Scare Ships.

At first, many believed the Scare Ships were German zeppelins sent over England to spy on British military installations. This theory was flawed, though. Zeppelins were still in their infancy in 1909; very few even existed then, and most of those were capable only of tethered flight. None could navigate a 700-mile round trip to the British Isles and back in the dead of night.

Plus, at its best, a zeppelin could fly about 50 miles an hour. Hundreds of witnesses saw the Scare Ships moving at more than 200 mph. They also saw them displaying their bright searchlights, weighty items to carry aboard a blimp.

Besides, if the Scare Ships *were* German spy platforms, why would they have operated in such a way that so many people saw them?

So what were they? Just like mysterious airships seen over America in 1896-97, and subsequent sightings over Australia, Russia, Poland, Austria, and Belgium in 1913, the Scare Ships have never been explained.

The Ghost Fliers

One night in late November 1933, residents across the vast Vasterbotten region of Sweden saw a large airplane, flying almost suicidally low, twisting its way through the area's rugged mountain valleys.

Eyewitnesses described the mystery craft as having eight-engines, a twin boom tail and pontoons, and carrying two huge searchlights.

The next night it happened again. The strange aircraft returned over Vasterbotten, searchlights blazing, engines roaring. The night after that, more mysterious aircraft were reported over the region — and the following night brought even more. Within a week, people were seeing the mysterious airplanes not just over Sweden, but over Norway and Finland as well. They were soon dubbed the Ghost Fliers.

They were almost always observed doing very odd things. Many times, the huge planes were spotted with their beacons illuminated, circling a village, a railroad station, or a mountaintop, bathing it in light. Another truly bizarre Ghost Flier antic was to sometimes turn off their engines while circling a village. In many cases, the residents would be outside looking up at the strange visitor and hear the plane's engines suddenly stop, only to restart again a few seconds later.

They were also able to fly in all kinds of weather, including blizzards, conditions that would keep other airplanes on the ground. And there was definitely more than just one of them. On some days, Ghost Fliers were reported in parts of southern *and* northern Sweden simultaneously. Sometimes they were even seen flying in formations.

What were the Ghost Fliers? Many people thought they were Nazi spy planes launched from a top-secret German aircraft carrier hidden in the Arctic Sea. But Nazi Germany never had an operational aircraft carrier.

And even if the Germans *were* able to launch a dozen or more aircraft at sea, at night, in brutal sub-polar conditions, doing it every day for what turned out to be many months would have been a titanic and grueling undertaking that surely would have caught the attention of many.

And if they were spy planes, what could they possibly have been looking for? The Arctic Circle region of Scandinavia is so isolated that even now it barely boasts more than one person per square mile.

So, like the Scare Ships, the Ghost Fliers remain a mystery.

The Ghost Rockets

No sooner had World War II ended that, once again, unidentified aerial objects began showing up over the Scandinavian Arctic.

The unexplained intruders weren't ghostly airplanes this time, but strange rockets seen streaking across the skies of Sweden, Norway, and Finland. As with the Ghost Fliers, many people saw them, including military pilots. On some days, literally hundreds were reported flying overhead.

Most intriguing, not only did many people see these objects flying horizontally — belying the theory that they were just meteors — they were also observed doing maneuvers, including pulling 180-degree turns and two or more flying in formation.

They were soon coined the Ghost Rockets, and unlike back in the early 1930s, when media coverage of the Ghost Fliers was somewhat muted and provincial, news of the Ghost Rockets went around the world in a flash.

While there were varying descriptions of the Ghost Rockets, one image became predominant: a fast-moving, missile-shaped object twelve to fifteen feet long with wings.

The Swedish government became so concerned about these airborne intruders that it violated the country's famous neutrality and secretly implored Great Britain to provide them with modern radar systems. Once these were in place, the result was astounding. More than *two hundred* of the Ghost Rockets were eventually tracked on radar.

One theory was the Ghost Rockets were actually Russian-updates of captured German V-1 buzz bombs and that the Soviets were using the former Nazi base at Peenemunde, 200 miles south of Sweden, to launch them.

But while Peenemunde had been overrun by the Russian Army near the end of World War II, by that time the rocket facility was in ruins from intensive Allied bombing.

Moreover, even in the best of times, the Germans could barely launch fifteen V-1 buzz bombs in a day. There were more than 200 Ghost Rocket sightings reported on July 9, 1946, alone. And on August 11 that year, more than *three hundred* of the strange objects were seen going over Stockholm.

Ghost Rocket sightings lasted throughout 1946. In all, about 2,000 were spotted from May to December that year. Then just like the Ghost Fliers, the Ghost Rockets just faded away.

So what were they?

On the morning of August 14, 1946, a Swedish Air Force pilot was flying over central Sweden when he saw an object soaring along slightly above him. It was one of the Ghost Rockets and it was traveling about 400 mph.

The pilot reported that not only was the object maintaining stable, horizontal flight, it was basically following the terrain, meaning if a mountain loomed before it, it simply climbed enough to clear the mountain before returning to its previous altitude. Known today as terrain-following guidance technology, it's something that wasn't even attempted until the 1960s — and not perfected until the 1980s.

Eric Malmberg was secretary of Sweden's Defense Staff committee during the time of the Ghost Rockets. He said later on: "If the observations were correct, many details suggest that it was some kind of a cruise missile. But nobody had that kind of sophisticated technology in 1946."

The Scare Ships, the Ghost Fliers and the Ghost Rockets. Three unusual kinds of UFOs. Three mysteries that have yet to be solved.

But all three appeared to share one thing in common: All seemed to make use of technologies way before their time.

Secret Bases Around the World

Nevada's Area 51 is the world's best-known secret base.

It's been featured in books, movies, and TV mostly because many people suspect the U.S. government hides UFOs there. But there are other places around the world like Area 51 — places that are truly secret and almost unknown, but with connections to UFOs as well. Some of these connections border on the ridiculous. But others are fascinating and truly baffling. A sampling follows:

S4, Nevada

Some researchers claim that S4, said to be located inside a desert mountain about twenty miles south of Area 51, is an enormous underground facility where the U.S. military builds its own flying saucers based on technology from crashed UFOs it has recovered over the years.

But others think S4 is a complete fabrication created by the CIA to fool Russian satellites into photographing nothing but empty desert.

San Luis Valley, Colorado

As mentioned earlier, Colorado's San Luis Valley is a place where UFOs are spotted on a regular basis and paranormal activity such as ghosts, "shadow people," unexplained lights, strange animals, and even flying humans have been reported as well.

The valley is located close to a number of highly classified military installations. Could they be the reason for all the spooky activity?

Archuleta Mesa, New Mexico

Some claim this mountain in Dulce, New Mexico, is home to 50,000 reptile-like aliens who, with the approval of the U.S. government, perform ghastly experiments on human beings with the ultimate purpose of enslaving mankind to work in plutonium mines on the moon and Mars.

Others say Archuleta Mesa is the greatest tall story in the history of UFOs, a fabrication created by members of the U.S. Air Force to misdirect UFO researchers.

As crazy as it sounds, the debate goes on.

Tonopah, Nevada

About 70 miles northwest of Area 51 is a place so secret, even people in the U.S. intelligence community rarely talk about it.

It's called the Tonopah Test Range, and the F-117 Stealth fighter was kept under wraps there for ten years without anybody but the president and the highest reaches of the U.S. military knowing about it. The Stealth fighters left Tonopah years ago, but the highly secret base is still open and operating.

This begs the question: What's being kept there now?

Tonopah, Arizona

Strangely, almost no UFOs are reported over Tonopah, Nevada. However, five hundred miles to the southeast is Tonopah, *Arizona,* where dramatic UFO sightings happen all the time.

These include reports of gigantic aerial ships seen accompanied by fighter planes and at least one dramatic encounter between a UFO's occupants and local citizens.

The Palo Verde nuclear plant, the largest of its kind in the world, is close by, and many people believe this is what attracts all the UFOs.

Homestead AFB, Florida

Located south of Miami, Homestead Air Force Base is the site of one of the most intriguing stories in UFO lore.

One night in 1974, President Richard Nixon brought his golfing buddy, comedian Jackie Gleason, to a highly classified hangar at Homestead. After swearing Gleason to secrecy, Nixon showed him the remains of a crashed flying saucer and the bodies of its crew.

Gleason was a well-known UFO enthusiast and the episode affected him deeply. Later on, when Gleason's wife alluded to the incident in a magazine article, Jackie ended their marriage.

But is the story true?

AUTEC

Officially known as the Atlantic Underwater Testing & Evaluation Center, and ostensibly a place where new technologies are assessed for America's nuclear submarine force, many UFO researchers insist AUTEC is really the U.S. Navy's "Area 51."

Not only have many UFOs been reported in its vicinity over the years, but hundreds of "USOs" (Unidentified Submerged Objects) have been seen near this super-secret facility as well.

The Navy denies all this, of course, but maybe the most mysterious thing about AUTEC is that it's located on the Bahamian island of Andros, which puts it right in the middle of the Bermuda Triangle.

England's Phantom Town

Until fairly recently, the village of Argleton, located in West Lancashire, England, had everything expected of a small British town.

It had its own postal code and appeared on Google maps. It had want ads for new jobs, an extensive real estate listing, its own weather report and even a local dating service.

Trouble was, Argleton didn't exist. In fact, it never existed. Anyone who went to the land coordinates given on Google would have found an empty field.

How did this happen?

One British newspaper said, "Google and the company that supplies its mapping data are unable to explain the presence of the phantom town."

Then—just as mysteriously as it materialized, the town disappeared. As of January 30, 2010, Argleton was wiped from all Google maps.

What does all this mean? There's no way of telling. There were no UFOs reported near the place, nor were there any signs of military activity in the area.

But as one intelligence veteran told us, "What better place for a government to hide secrets than in a town that never existed?"

Britain's Area 51

Great Britain is a crowded island with few places to put a top-secret Area 51-type base. However, many researchers believe Britain's Area 51 can be found beneath a stately English mansion called Rudloe Manor.

A small city was constructed underneath the manor during World War II as a place to build fighter planes away from falling German bombs. Wouldn't this be the perfect place for Britain's military to hide modern-day secret weapons and maybe even crashed UFOs?

Even more intriguing, Rudloe Manor is located close to Salisbury Plain, the site of Stonehenge.

Saddam's Area 51

When the invasion of Iraq began in March 2003, U.S. forces paid particular attention to a place called the Little Zab River Valley. After bombing it frequently, scores of

Special Forces troops were sent in to search the area west of Baghdad.

The valley was reportedly the site of what many called "Saddam's Area 51." Ever since the first Gulf War there have been reports that Saddam's forces had recovered a crashed UFO, brought it to the Little Zab River Valley, reverse-engineered some of its technology, and from this, created a supply of extraterrestrial-inspired weapons of mass destruction.

Could this be the elusive WMD U.S. forces were looking for?

Wenceslas Mine, Poland

Located in southwest Poland, this facility has long been rumored to be the site of a secret World War II program to build a propulsion unit for Nazi UFOs.

True believers say the technology for this mysterious device, known as "The Bell," came from a highly advanced alien civilization that was in cahoots with Hitler and the Third Reich.

However, more rational researchers point out that if the Nazis truly had superior technological help from ETs, why did they lose the war?

Kapustin Yar, Russia

Kapustin Yar is a combination space launch facility and secret weapons base operated by the Russian armed forces. Many sources inside Russia, including famous pilots and aeronautical experts, insist that Russian fighter jets and UFOs engaged in numerous dogfights over the base after UFOs attempted to interfere with some early Russian missile launches.

Aksai Chin

People in this remote area in the Himalayan Mountains on the border of China and India claim to regularly see UFOs coming out of deep ravines and crevices.

These sightings are so frequent that when children in the area were asked to draw something from their everyday lives, many of them drew pictures of flying saucer-like objects.

China and India fought a war over this snowy region in 1962, and these days, both governments restrict access to this mysterious corner of the world.

Pine Gap, Australia

Considered one of the most secret places on Earth, Pine Gap is located at the geographic dead center of Australia. It is from here that the National Security Agency controls America's latest fleet of spy satellites, many of which eavesdrop on other nations and individuals.

But Pine Gap is also known for some spectacular UFO sightings during which witnesses report seeing interaction between UFO occupants and personnel at the base.

Could the U.S. have drones operating from Pine Gap that are disguised to look like UFOs?

Weirdness in Real Life:
Mack in the Movies

One day I saw a notice in a Boston newspaper announcing a casting call.

A film company was looking for extras to appear in a movie starring John Travolta. A few scenes were to be filmed in Fenway Park, and all the extras would be portraying Red Sox fans.

My wife is very photogenic, and I was convinced that the movie people would put her in the film. It took me two days to convince her to go down to Fenway Park (about an hour from where we live) for the casting call. Finally, just to shut me up, she agreed and down we went.

The casting call was being held at a huge nightclub next to the park. There were about 5,000 people already inside, and this was the third day of casting! My wife went through the process, filling out forms, having her picture taken, and so on — essentially an afternoon spent waiting in long lines.

I stayed with her as she went from one station to another. At one point, a guy walked up to me and handed me a red ticket. He told me: "Hold on to this; an announcement will be made soon." Then he walked away. I thought they were giving away a door prize or something.

Eventually, we all filed into a huge room where the producers explained to the masses that if anyone still wanted to be an extra, they would have to go to Fenway Park the following Monday at 6 a.m. in summer clothes (this was late October) and be prepared to sit around for three days — all for $40 and a box lunch.

This was not for my wife, so we got up to go when the producers announced that anyone with a red ticket should stay behind. In this huge room, just two African-American women and I had red tickets. We had no idea what was going on.

The two women were whisked away, so it was just my wife and me sitting alone in this big room. Finally, another producer arrived. He thanked me for hanging around and said he wanted *me* to be in the movie. Was I interested in playing a part?

I thought it was a joke, but he said I had "a look" they needed. They couldn't tell me what the part was (it wasn't for the Fenway Park scenes) but would give me more information if I was interested. I couldn't believe it was happening — neither could my wife. So, even though I was writing a book on deadline, I agreed.

I had my picture taken a bunch of times and filled out numerous forms. After all this hoopla I was convinced I was going to be playing John Travolta's best friend. Once

I was processed, the producer told me his company in Hollywood would call me the following week.

Sure enough, the call came late one night. They said they still couldn't tell me what part I was to play, but that I should get to a place in Woburn, Massachusetts, about 40 minutes from where we live, at 6 the next morning, and that I should "wear warm clothes you don't expect to ever wear again." That was the first indication that I wasn't being cast as Travolta's sidekick.

I showed up on the movie set the next day (actually, it was an abandoned state mental facility) to find hundreds of Hollywood people, extras, lights, cameras, Teamsters - - a huge production. I was processed yet again, pictures taken, more forms filled out. I was dressed in very old clothes, as instructed. Eventually I was told to wait in a trailer with about two dozen other guys, all my age, all of them also wearing old clothes.

Frankly, though, these guys all looked like they'd just been let out of prison. Broken noses, missing teeth, scars, tattoos. A roomful of penitentiary faces. If there were any mirrors around, they would have broken on the spot.

Finally, a producer told us why we were here: We were all going to play workers in a factory that was illegally disposing hazardous waste. The movie was titled "A Civil Action," and was about a crusading lawyer (John Travolta) who stops the factory from dumping pollutants into Woburn's water supply — a true story, by the way. But in other words, we were going to be the bad guys.

We were all sent to the wardrobe trailer, where they checked to see if our clothes were crappy enough for the movie. The trailer was run by two gay guys right out of central casting. They took one look at me and started screaming: "Complete makeover!" I was pulled out of line and put in even crappier clothes. They told me I'd have to pay for them if I lost them.

What followed was a string of very long, very cold days basically hanging around waiting for cameras, lights, etc., etc. It was freezing out (it was November by this time), but I got lucky the first day when they picked me to be one of two guys in a truck that was supposed to drive through a huge scene where hazardous waste was being smuggled out of the plant.

There were about 50 people in the scene, so it took a long time to set up and choreograph — and two days to shoot. We did this truck-driving scene at least 40 times each day. Again, I was lucky because I was able to sit inside the truck between takes. We had the heater going full blast and were able to listen to the radio.

The guy who was playing the driver was a human bowling ball who was all over Boston TV at the time playing a construction worker in Ford commercials. His name was Bob Dugan, another Boston Irishman, and a really nice guy. I still see him in TV ads occasionally.

When we weren't needed outside, all us mug faces sat in the cafeteria and played poker. They fed us three times a day — they call it Craft Services in the biz — and the food was outstanding.

We all got to meet John Travolta. Before this, he'd always seemed like a typical Hollywood asshole to me, but I've got to say he was really down to Earth with us. He made sure he met and shook hands with every extra on the set, and he always talked to us if we happened to run into him walking around. After a while, people were turning up with stuff for him to autograph — record albums and things — and he was always very accommodating.

I worked five days over the next couple of weeks. I got paid $110 a day and won another $100 or so playing cards. As I was leaving on the last day, the casting director called me aside and asked if I was available for other work. I asked him for what kind of movies. He said, "Bar scenes and prison scenes, exclusively." (See a pattern forming here?) I said sure, call my people.

The movie came out about a year later. One-third of the way into the film, there's a scene where Travolta walks up from some woods and sees the waste plant with barrels of pollutants scattered all over. A truck drives by the camera. I'm the passenger in that truck.

Total screen time: 1.2 seconds.

Celebrity UFO Sightings

William Shatner

Beam him up, somebody …

William Shatner once claimed a UFO saved his life after his motorcycle broke down in the Mojave Desert. He was stranded and without water in 130-degree heat when a mysterious object suddenly appeared in the sky and guided him to a gas station and to safety.

But Shatner later recanted the story in his autobiography, telling The New York Times, "I told the truth that I lied."

Mick Jagger

While camping in Glastonbury in 1968 with then-girlfriend Marianne Faithful, Mick Jagger spotted what he described as a "cigar-shaped mothership" floating among the stars.

A year later, the Rolling Stones front man saw a second UFO during the infamous concert at Altamont. The sightings left such an impression on the singer he installed a "UFO detector" at his English estate. (Most mysterious part of this story: Mick Jagger goes camping?)

John Lennon

In August 1974, ex-Beatle John Lennon was on the roof of his New York City apartment when he saw a disk-shaped UFO hovering just a hundred feet away. His girlfriend at the time, May Pang, was able to grab a camera and take a few photos of the object before it took off. But when the film was developed, all the pictures came out blank.

Jimmy Carter

In 1969, future president Jimmy Carter was standing outside a Lion's Club in Leary, Georgia, when he and a small group of people observed a brilliant, multi-colored light shining in the night sky.

Like any good doobee, Mr. Peanut filed a UFO report on the incident, but experts later said what Carter saw was the planet Venus.

Ronald Reagan

Ronald Reagan saw a UFO while he was governor of California.

Traveling aboard his personal plane in the summer of 1974, Reagan spotted a strange object flying outside his window. At Reagan's suggestion, the pilot followed the UFO for a few minutes before it suddenly went straight up and disappeared in a flash.

Muhammad Ali

Jogging in New York's Central Park one day, boxing legend Muhammad Ali saw a bright light suddenly appear over his head and start moving along with him.

But this was no big deal for the Champ, who claimed to have seen many UFOs in his lifetime. "If you look up in the sky in the early morning," he once said, "you see them playing tag between the stars."

David Bowie

While traveling through the English countryside one day, rock star David Bowie spotted a UFO hovering over a field. From that moment on, he became hooked … on something.

Said Bowie, "I believe that what I saw was not an object, but a projection of my own mind trying to make some sense of this quantum topological doorway into dimensions beyond our own."

Got that, Major Tom?

Dan Aykroyd

Longtime UFO buff Dan Aykroyd might own the most famous ET "non-sighting."

It happened back in the '80s, when the SNL funnyman woke up in the middle of the night and told his wife,

"They are calling me; I want to go outside." But his wife suggested he go back to sleep instead.

The next day, people all over upstate New York reported having the same urge to go outside at three in the morning. Those who heeded the call saw a tremendously large pink spiral object hovering in the sky.

Alexander the Great

The renowned radio commentator Frank Edwards once told a story about Alexander the Great having an unearthly encounter during his bid to conquer the known world.

In 332 B.C., Alexander's huge army had come to a strategic river crossing. The Macedonian mastermind had to swiftly move his forces across the waterway to continue his campaign. But just as he was about to ford the river, two strange craft suddenly appeared in the sky.

Alexander's own historian described the craft as shining silvery shields with arrows of fire spitting from their rims. As Alexander watched in horror, the strange craft dove repeatedly at his men to the point where they, their horses, and his war elephants became so panicked, they refused to cross the river.

Christopher Columbus

On the night of October 12, 1492, Christopher Columbus was on the deck of his ship, the *Santa Maria*, gazing out on the dark Atlantic.

Suddenly he saw a light glimmering in the distance. The light began moving up and down and flashing with such intensity, it kept the explorer's eyes locked on the horizon.

About four hours after first seeing the strange light, Columbus spotted land.

15 Weird Facts About Roswell

1. On or about the night of July 4, 1947, a disk-shaped object was reported streaking through the sky above Roswell, New Mexico, then a small city in the southeastern part of the state. A severe thunderstorm was passing through the area at the time, and some residents recalled hearing a loud explosion at the height of the storm.

2. The next day, a rancher came forward to say he'd found bits of strange-looking wreckage scattered across an open field about seventy-five miles northwest of Roswell. He described the wreckage as shiny metallic material, similar to tin foil, and balsa-like wooden sticks cut in the shape of I-beams.

3. Others who later handled this debris claimed it possessed incredible properties. The metallic material had super strength and the ability to "unfold itself." The beams were impossible to break or burn. They also had indecipherable "hieroglyphics" printed on them.

4. The military was alerted to the rancher's discovery. The wreckage was collected and taken to nearby Roswell Army Air Field, where the base's intelligence officers

examined it. On July 8, the base's public affairs officer issued a startling press release declaring the wreckage had come from a flying saucer. This announcement made headlines across the country.

5. In July 1947, people from every state in the union were reporting "flying saucers," a term we know was coined just weeks earlier by pilot Kenneth Arnold after he'd spotted a group of saucer-shaped objects passing over the Cascade Mountains in Washington State. With the military's announcement in Roswell, it seemed as if the flying saucer mystery was about to be solved.

6. But later on July 8, the military issued another press statement saying the wreckage was not from a flying saucer, but from a harmless weather balloon. Most people believed this version, and the Roswell crash story went away for more than thirty years.

7. In 1978, a UFO researcher interviewed Major Jesse Marcel, an Air Force officer who had been involved in recovering the original Roswell debris. Marcel stated for the first time that he believed the debris was from an alien spacecraft and that the U.S. military had covered up the crash. Marcel told the same story to the *National Enquir-*

er two years later, thrusting the Roswell incident back into the headlines.

8. After the *National Enquirer* story appeared, a number of people from the Roswell area came forward claiming they'd seen alien bodies taken from the crash site 33 years before. Because Roswell Army Air Field was home to the 509th Bomb Group, the only Air Force unit equipped with atomic weapons at the time, some UFO researchers theorized that the wrecked flying saucer had been shot down while spying on America's sole nuclear weapons base. Other UFO proponents claim more than a dozen UFOs have crashed at Roswell over the years and that more than two dozen alien bodies have been recovered there.

9. The renewed interest in the Roswell Incident caused an explosion of books, documentary films, TV programs — even a cartoon show, "Roswell Conspiracies, Aliens, Myths and Legends." The premise of this 1999 animated series was that the Roswell crash was a manmade event orchestrated by the government to deflect attention from the fact that aliens had been living among us for centuries.

10. A little-known Roswell fact has to do with what happened to the 509th Bomb Group in the years following the Roswell incident. The nuclear-armed bomber unit left Roswell in 1958 and found a new home at Pease Air Force Base in Portsmouth, New Hampshire. Almost immediately, UFO sightings around Portsmouth and the surrounding area skyrocketed, a trend that some UFO researchers say continues today.

11. In 1984, memos supposedly originating from a classified operation concerning Roswell mysteriously surfaced. Called the Majestic 12 documents, it was claimed that they came from secret meetings held by President Harry Truman to "handle" the Roswell incident. However, the memos were later determined to be fakes, and there's no credible evidence that anything called Majestic 12 ever existed.

12. The U.S. Air Force issued two reports on the Roswell incident in the 1990s. The first report, released in 1995, concluded that the material recovered in 1947 was likely debris from a balloon used in a top-secret operation called Project Mogul, which deployed high-altitude balloons to spy on Russia's nuclear capabilities. The second report, released in 1997, concluded that recollections of recovered alien bodies were likely transformed

memories of military accidents combined with the recovery of lifelike dummies used in high-altitude research programs the military was conducting in the area at the time. However, these reports were dismissed by many UFO proponents who claimed the military cover-up was still ongoing.

13. Some UFO researchers say a UFO "crash" near Aztec, New Mexico, eight months after Roswell has more hard evidence and more credible eyewitnesses than the Roswell incident itself. In early March 1948, oil workers near Aztec saw a disk crash close to their oil rigs. They were able to look inside the disk and reportedly saw the dead bodies of its non-human crew. The military arrived and took the disk away using a huge crane, but before doing so, had to lay a cement foundation pad in the desert to support the crane's weight. While some UFO researchers dismiss what has become known as "the other Roswell" as a hoax, others insist the story is true and that the concrete pad used in the flying saucer's recovery is still there.

14. In 2012, a retired CIA officer named Chase Brandon claimed he'd seen evidence confirming that an alien spacecraft had crashed at Roswell in 1947 and that the U.S. government has been covering it up ever since.

Brandon said he'd gotten access to a normally off-limits part of CIA headquarters in Langley, Virginia, and that documents he found there convinced him that not only did a UFO crash at Roswell, but that remains of its occupants were found. Brandon's assertions were dampened, however, by the fact that at the time he was promoting a science fiction novel he'd written about a CIA cover-up of the Roswell incident.

15. Roswell's residents have not been shy about cashing in on the crash controversy. The no-longer-small city has become a major tourist attraction. It's home to a UFO museum and an annual UFO festival. In recent years, this festival has included dozens of speeches on crop circles, ghosts, angels, how the occult and UFOs are connected, and how a person would know if he or she had been abducted by aliens. There's also a fireworks extravaganza and entertainment from a number of music groups, including one called Cosmic Sucker Punch.

After all these years, whatever happened at Roswell remains a mystery in more ways than one.

15 REALLY Weird Things About Outer Space

1. Gamma-ray bursts, caused by things like two black holes colliding, are so powerful, they can destroy all life on any planet at any time from thousands of light-years away.

2. The planet 55 Cancri e, located 48 light-years from Earth, is made entirely of diamond.

3. The center of our galaxy smells like rum and raspberries. Google *ethyl formate*.

4. Some stars speed through space at more than 20 million miles an hour.

5. Don't think size matters? Think again. Not only is there the Himiko Cloud, which at more than half the size of the Milky Way is one of the largest objects in the universe, but there's an electrical current — basically a single, long electrical bolt — coming from a black hole nearby that's 1.5 times longer than the width of the Milky Way.

6. You cannot cry in space. In zero gravity, your tears turn into little balls of liquid that irritate your eyes before they float away.

7. The Martian volcano *Olympus Mons* is 16 miles high. Its top measures 50 miles across and its base takes up more than 100,000 square miles, roughly the same size of as the state of Arizona.

8. A star called R136a1 is 256 times bigger than our sun and shines 7.4 million times brighter.

9. The Bootes Void is an empty section of space that contains only sixty or so galaxies where normally 20,000 galaxies should be. The laws of physics say that, as we understand our universe at the moment, this is not possible. One explanation for the void, which is 330 million light-years in diameter, is that a super-advanced race has surrounded the missing stars with Dyson Shells, mega-structures that would allow them to use the stars' energy while hiding them from view.

10. If you were somehow able to hang in space and witness a star exploding, you would hear no sound, because sound doesn't travel in space.

11. Because the moon has no wind and no atmosphere, the footprints of the lunar astronauts will remain there unchanged for at least the next hundred million years.

12. By conservative estimates, there are one hundred billion trillion stars in the universe. If just 0.0000000001 percent of them can support life, that would mean there are 600 billion alien worlds out there.

13. There's a trio of craters on Mercury that looks exactly like the Mickey Mouse logo.

14. America's lunar astronauts left 400,000 pounds of trash behind on the moon.

15. There has been a human burial on the moon. Eugene Shoemaker, the scientist who co-discovered the Shoemaker-Levy comet, had always wanted to be an astronaut but was prevented from doing so for medical reasons. When he died in 1997, friends inside NASA pulled some strings and arranged for Shoemaker's ashes to be carried to the moon aboard the Lunar Prospector Orbiter.

At the end of the orbiter's mission, NASA intentionally crashed it into the moon, scattering Shoemaker's ashes across the lunar landscape.

Ghosts & Airplanes

Looking Down Through Time

One day in 1934, RAF Air Marshal Sir Victor Goddard was flying a Hawker Hart bomber over Scotland through heavy mist and rain. Looking for a landmark to guide him home, he reduced his altitude, hoping to see an abandoned airfield he knew was near the village of Drem, about twenty miles east of Edinburgh.

Breaking through the clouds, he spotted the airfield, but to his astonishment, it was bathed in sunlight. He could clearly see yellow aircraft lined up on the tarmac and technicians in blue overalls tending to them. Even though he was flying very low by this time, no one on the ground bothered to look up as he roared overhead. Baffled, Goddard continued homeward.

Four years later, with World War II looming on the horizon, the airfield at Drem was reopened as a training base. For the first time, RAF training aircraft were painted yellow for easy identification, and new uniforms given to their ground crews were colored bright blue.

When Goddard learned of all this, he realized the only explanation for his 1934 incident was that, for some reason, he'd been given a glimpse of the future.

The Ghost Plane of 1933

One of New York state's oldest unsolved mysteries is the Ghost Plane of 1933.

On the afternoon of December 26, during a brutal snowstorm, every airfield in the greater New York City area was asked to turn on its landing lights in hopes that an airplane heard circling the city might be able to land.

Attempts to contact the plane by radio had failed; no one knew who was flying it or where it had come from.

Workers in Manhattan skyscrapers were the first to hear the plane's drone. By nightfall, the NYPD was fielding numerous calls from people seeing an airplane flying dangerously close to the ground, as if looking for a place to land.

But then the ghost airplane simply disappeared. It did not land at any airport in the area and no crashes were reported, nor were any airplanes or pilots ever reported missing.

Ethereal Passengers

On December 29, 1972, Eastern Air Lines Flight 401 crashed into the Florida Everglades while trying to land at Miami International Airport. The accident killed 101 people, including the pilot and the flight engineer.

The doomed plane was a three-engine L-1011 Tri-Star wide-body, a fairly new design. After the crash, the ghosts of the pilot and engineer were reportedly seen on more than twenty occasions aboard other Eastern Air Lines flights. Witnesses included people who had known both men as well as others who identified them from photographs later on.

The ghosts, who appeared as being wholly lifelike, were most frequently seen aboard other Tri-Stars that had been fitted with parts salvaged from the Flight 401 crash.

Although Eastern's management later called the ghost stories "garbage," all parts taken from Flight 401 were eventually removed from other Eastern aircraft.

The Ghost of Biggin Hill

The Spitfire fighter plane is one of the most famous aircraft ever, recognized for its contribution in winning the Battle of Britain against Germany in World War II. Its Merlin engine has a very distinctive sound, unmistakable to those familiar with it.

There is an airfield in Kent, England, called Biggin Hill. Spitfires assigned to this frontline base flew up to a dozen missions a day in the late summer and early fall of 1940, trying to stop the Nazis' aerial onslaught. After the war, the Spitfires remained at the base until the early

1950s, when they were finally moved out and eventually retired.

More than 20,000 Spitfires were built between 1938 and 1948. As of this writing, just thirty are still in flying condition in the U.K., most of them safely ensconced in private hangars and each one accounted for.

So how to explain what has happened above Biggin Hill on more than a few occasions when witnesses see a Spitfire fly over the base, perform a victory roll, and then disappear again? This inexplicable sight has been reported by local residents, fire and rescue crews, law enforcement, and former pilots.

So many people have seen, and still see, the ghost airplane that the RAF had to issue the following statement: "Too many rational people have reported it for it to be a hoax, and it's certainly not another make of airplane that has been mistaken for a Spitfire."

Mystery at Palmyra

One night in late June 1944, a Coast Guard vessel sailing about 800 miles southeast of Hawaii received an urgent radio message. A U.S. Navy patrol plane had crashed into the sea close to its location. The Coast Guard ship was asked to search for survivors.

Immediately changing course, the Coast Guard vessel rushed to the suspected crash area and used its searchlights to look for any wreckage or survivors. They found nothing.

A day later, the ship was anchored at the nearby island of Palmyra. Its executive officer was on the bridge, standing watch around midnight, when he spotted a bright light over the island.

The light began to grow, even as he was watching it, coming closer every second. For a moment, the XO thought this might be the lost patrol plane, somehow returning home. But on looking at the light through binoculars, the XO realized it was no typical aircraft, lost or otherwise.

It was a sphere, perfectly round, and very bright. It eventually went into a near-hover above the Coast Guard ship, moving so slowly that at times, it appeared to be stopped in midair.

This went on for more than thirty minutes until the sphere finally picked up speed and moved off to the north, in the same direction where the patrol plane had been lost.

The next day, the XO had a conversation with a Navy lieutenant concerning the missing plane and the otherworldly sphere.

The fact that the patrol plane was missing was a huge mystery for everyone involved. Its crew was well trained and experienced. When flying over large areas of water, long-range pilots relied on their direction-finders to be in working condition. But even if the lost plane's gear had malfunctioned, the pilots would have known which direction they were heading simply by noting the position of the setting sun.

As for the sphere, the Navy officer told the XO that no U.S. planes had been up the night before, and there wasn't a Japanese plane within 1,000 miles of the island. So whatever the XO saw, it didn't belong to either side.

In telling the story later, the XO admitted he believed the two incidents — the lost plane and the unearthly sphere — were related. The Navy lieutenant had seconded that theory.

The missing plane was never found.

The Galloping Ghosts of Nansei Shoto

The Nansei Shoto archipelago is located off the southern coast of Japan.

It's a strange part of the world, a patch of mostly water and a few volcanic islands, one being Okinawa. After sailing through it, though, many sailors — including those in the U.S. Navy during World War II — became convinced this part of the Pacific was haunted by something, though no one was really sure what.

For instance, American submarines plying its waters would sometimes pick up sonar indications of ghostly ships that just weren't there. These things caused much consternation for the Navy's silent service, especially when operating so close to the Japanese Home Islands. A popular science magazine explained it this way: A submarine radar man would monitor his scope, his radar antenna riding just above the surface while the sub itself was riding just below. Suddenly the radar man would pick up an indication that something looking like an enemy vessel was heading for his submarine. If the radar man warned that a change in course was needed, the indication would turn exactly how the sub was turning.

The sub's captain would inevitably go up-periscope and take the chance of scanning the sea's surface for the enemy warship. But then, just as suddenly, the indication would vanish from the radar screen.

Thus the name "ghosts."

Many theories were put forth on what these things were — mirages, cold-weather inversions, and "air sandwiches" — freakish conditions resulting when low-lying cold air traps radar signals. But no satisfactory explanation has ever been proven.

These spirits didn't spook just submarines. The so-called "Galloping Ghosts of Nansei Shoto" also shadowed the U.S. surface fleet and were especially troublesome to aircraft carriers. On many occasions, night fighters would be scrambled to intercept the ghostly electronic indications, but no plane ever got close enough to engage what was showing up on the radar screens.

These particular radar mirages were thought at first to be some kind of secret weapon the Japanese were testing, a concern that, for good reason, went right to the top of the Navy brass.

In the summer of 1945 a radar operator on an aircraft carrier steaming near the Nansei Shoto archipelago saw a "very large plot" suddenly appear on his radar screen. Incredibly, it looked like *300* unidentified aircraft were heading for the carrier. Even crazier, this mass of aircraft seemed to be traveling at nearly 700 mph — much faster than any airplane, on either side, could go in 1945.

Two Navy fighters were immediately scrambled, and this is where it got *really* got weird.

About sixty-five miles from the carrier, the very large plot of targets began morphing into what were later described as "tentacles." The radar screen showed these tentacles wrapping themselves around the carrier!

The two fighters were madly flying toward the target as the entire task force waited apprehensively below.

But when the fighters reached the point indicated on the radar, they found nothing. The large plot had simply disappeared.

No explanation has ever been given for the strange occurrence.

The Thunderscreech

Back in 1955, the U.S. Air Force came up with an odd idea: use a jet engine to spin a propeller. Airplane designers went to work and created the XF-84 Thunderscreech fighter, so-called due to the ungodly noise it made whenever it took flight. Because the propeller spun faster than the speed of sound, it was by far the loudest plane ever built, with its engine heard starting up from twenty-five miles away.

However, the sonic waves the aircraft gave off were *so* powerful that they blew out eardrums, caused nausea and vomiting, and in some cases even provoked epileptic seizures among ground crews. The Thunderscreech project was canceled just a year later.

The Empty Cockpit

One of the oddest ghost plane mysteries ever happened in March, 2017.

Authorities in Marathon, Ontario, Canada, received a report that a Cessna 172 flying out of Michigan had crashed near the north shore of Lake Superior shortly before midnight.

But when local rescue teams reached the crash site, they made a startling discovery. Not only was there no sign of the pilot; there weren't any footprints in the snow around the crashed plane, either.

So how did it get there?

And what happened to the person who was flying it?

The Swing-Wing Ghosts

The U.S.-built FB-111Aardvark was the first operational military swing-wing aircraft. It was designed as a fighter-bomber, and its pilots could adjust their wings forward for landings, midway back for normal flight, or flared all the way back for supersonic flight.

A technological marvel for its time, the FB-111 also employed an extremely advanced flight control system that allowed its pilots to fly very low in order to evade enemy radar.

Used mostly in Vietnam as a special-mission aircraft, an FB-111 took off from Udorn Air Force Base in northern Thailand one night for a sortie over communist North Vietnam.

By all accounts, the plane accomplished its mission but was hit by enemy ground fire on its return flight. All communications with the plane ceased, and it was given up as lost — one of several hundred American warplanes shot down during the war.

Yet just around the time it was due back at Udorn, the plane appeared on the base's radar screens. Astonished ground personnel watched as it landed and taxied over to its hangar.

But on opening its canopy, the air mechanics found both pilots dead, killed by shrapnel from an antiaircraft burst.

The plane's sophisticated flight controls, undamaged in the explosion, kept the aircraft flying and brought its pilots home.

The Right Stuff Ghost

Shortly before 8 a.m. on June 13, 1993, a bright-red Formula 1 speed-racer airplane appeared over the John Wayne Airport in Orange County, California.

A small plane with a huge engine, it made so much of a racket that it tripped the airport's noise monitoring systems, in place because the Wayne airport, being close to many residences, boasts one of the strictest airport noise abatement programs in the country.

As the midget racer began to fly various acrobatic maneuvers above the airport, enough people saw it to write down the ID number emblazoned on its fuselage. Then they watched as the plane, later confirmed as FAA-registered N21X, slowly climbed and disappeared over the Pacific.

Working with witnesses' information, airport officials sent a noise violation notice to the plane's owner, who just happened to be Deke Slayton, one of NASA's Original Seven Mercury astronauts and commander of the famous 1975 Apollo-Soyuz space mission.

What the airport officials didn't know was that Slayton had passed away five hours before, dying at his home in Houston, 1,500 miles from Orange County, with his wife and daughter at his bedside.

And his airplane was locked away in a hangar in Sparks, Nevada, whose owner later testified it had not been flown or even taken from its hangar since Slayton gave it to him a few years before.

No one has ever been able to explain the bizarre incident.

Ghost Ships

The Ourang Medan

On June 15, 1947, two ships sailing off the coast of Malaysia intercepted a strange radio message from the freighter, *Ourang Medan*.

Emerging from the static, a ghostly voice was saying, over and over, that the vessel was in imminent danger. Then the transmission abruptly ended.

When rescuers arrived, they found the *Ourang Medan* drifting aimlessly. Climbing aboard the boat, they found the bodies of the crew strewn on the deck, in cabins, and in the cargo holds below. Each victim had the same terrified expression frozen on his face. Many had died pointing upward, toward the sky.

Before the rescuers could make sense of this, the ship suddenly erupted in flames, forcing all to flee. It sank seconds later.

Though one rumor claimed a UFO had attacked the freighter, there's never been any official explanation for the ship's demise.

The Baychimo

Launched in 1920, the cargo steamer *Baychimo* was used for transporting pelts and furs along the coast of the American Northwest.

In the winter of 1931, she became hopelessly locked in an arctic icepack off Alaska, forcing the crew to abandon ship. Incredibly, though, the freighter somehow broke free of the ice and drifted, empty and abandoned, for the next 40 years.

The vessel was spotted many times by sailors and fishermen over those four decades. The last reported sighting of the ghost ship occurred in 1969 and, eerily, some who saw her that final time reported that the steamer appeared to have suffered little over the years. In fact, some claimed it resembled a newly built ship and not some lonely ghost ship wandering the sea.

The Eliza Battle

Built in 1852, the *Eliza Battle* was a luxurious steam-powered paddleboat that catered to wealthy travelers.

One night in February 1858, while sailing on Alabama's Tombigbee River, the boat caught fire and sank, killing twenty-six people, including many women and children.

Locals say that ever since, on nights with a full moon, the riverboat can be seen floating along the river, music still playing and fires still burning on its deck. Many believe that spotting the ghost ship signals bad omens for others sailing the Tombigbee.

The Joyita

On October 3, 1955, the luxury yacht *Joyita* set sail from American Samoa bound for the Tokelau Islands, two days away.

It never arrived.

While a massive search by the Royal New Zealand Air Force turned up nothing, five weeks later the vessel was found sailing more than six hundred miles off her original course. Her engines were still working and the navigation gear was still intact. But the twenty-five people on board, including the crew, had vanished without a trace.

While an official inquiry concluded the fate of the crew was "inexplicable," one persistent theory claims that Japanese soldiers, left over from World War II and hiding on a nearby island, attacked the yacht and killed everyone on board.

The Octavius

On October 11, 1775, while sailing off the west coast of Greenland, the whaling vessel *Herald* came upon a mysterious ship.

It was the *Octavius*, a British cargo vessel thought to have sunk more than a decade before. A party from the *Herald* climbed aboard the *Octavius* to find its entire crew frozen to death, including the captain, who was still sitting at his desk, hovering over the ship's log, his pen frozen in hand.

His partially completed log entry was dated early 1762, meaning the *Octavius* and its ice-encased crew had been drifting the waters of the far North Atlantic for thirteen years.

The SS Valencia

On January 22, 1906, while sailing in bad weather off the coast of Vancouver, British Columbia, the steamer *Valencia* struck a reef and began to sink.

Confusion ensued as, amid panicked cries from passengers for help, the steamer's crew tried to lower life rafts into the rough seas, causing several to capsize and one to disappear altogether. Of the 180 people on board, only 37 survived; the rest drowned or went missing.

Five months later, a local man exploring a cave near the site of the tragedy found the *Valencia's* missing life raft — with eight skeletons in it. How it got in the cave and how its occupants died is still a mystery.

But ever since, numerous sailors have reported seeing the ghostly steamer drifting near the reef where it went down, passengers still on its decks, still crying out for help.

The Aim High 6

On January 8, 2003, the Taiwanese fishing vessel *Aim High 6* was seen sailing peacefully off the west coast of Australia.

But when routine attempts to contact the ship failed, a rescue party went aboard only to find its crew had vanished.

The ship still had plenty of fuel and provisions aboard. None of the crew's personal belongings were missing, and no signs of a struggle were found.

While an extensive search turned up nothing of the crew, ten days after the ghost ship was discovered, mysterious calls were still being made on a cell phone belonging to the ship's engineer. Then they suddenly stopped as well.

Exactly what happened aboard *Aim High 6* has never been determined.

The Mary Celeste

Possibly the greatest maritime mystery ever, the case of the *Mary Celeste* has baffled historians for nearly 150 years.

On December 4, 1872, the British-American merchant ship was found drifting in the Atlantic, 600 miles west of Portugal. Its sails were up and functioning and there were plenty of provisions on board. The captain's log was intact and the personal belongings of the ten passengers and crew were untouched.

But the people on board had vanished.

Piracy was ruled out, as the ship had been carrying 1,500 barrels of alcohol that were found unmolested. Theories ranging from UFO abduction to sea monsters to an undersea earthquake have been considered, but no reasonable explanation has ever been found.

The Caleuche

Off the coast of southern Chile, near the island of Chiloe, locals swear a ghost ship named the *Caleuche* appears almost every night.

Described as strikingly beautiful, the ethereal sailing vessel is said to carry all the souls who have perished in the nearby seas over the years. When sighted, the *Caleuche* is always shining brightly, surrounded by multi-colored lights and accompanied by sounds of festive music and uproarious laughter.

But as soon as it's spotted, the ship quickly disappears.

The Lady Lovibond

On February 13, 1748, the captain of the British sailing vessel *Lady Lovibond* took his new bride on a sea voyage to celebrate their recent marriage.

However, seafaring legends say bringing a newlywed on a cruise invites bad luck, and that was the case for the *Lady Lovibond*.

Becoming overwhelmed with lust for his captain's new bride, the ship's first mate intentionally sank the *Lady Lovibond* off the coast of Kent, England, drowning all on board.

Since then, once every fifty years, the ship has been sighted sailing near the spot of its sinking, appearing as a vessel in distress. It seemed so real to one ship captain in 1898 that he dispatched a rescue party to help her before the apparition disappeared in the fog.

More Weirdness in Real Life:
Mack & the FBI

Remember the anthrax terrorist?

Right after 9/11, someone mailed packets of anthrax to a newspaper office in Florida, to some politicians in Washington, and to some network news anchors. Several people died as a result.

Both the FBI and the U.S. Postal Service were on the hunt for this guy. The post office was offering a $1 million reward for information that led to the terrorist's arrest. Any news show we watched during those days had a message running at the bottom, asking for the public's help in catching the killer.

One night I fell asleep watching the World Series and dreamt that whoever was mailing the deadly anthrax was probably doing it in his home somewhere. But because this stuff is so deadly, it was unlikely that he was packing envelopes over his kitchen sink or in his bathtub.

Even if he was wearing protective gear, he'd contaminate his house. Again, in the dream, it dawned on me that he was probably using a glovebox to pack the anthrax into the letters he was mailing.

A glovebox looks like a big home aquarium, but without the water and fish. They are made of thick glass and have two holes in one side through which heavy rubber gloves are placed. People put their hands in the gloves and are thus able to work with hazardous materials without contaminating themselves or their surroundings.

As it happened, my neighbor owned a company that made gloveboxes — one of only five such companies in the U.S. The next day I told him my theory and said that if anyone out of the ordinary had ordered a glovebox from his company recently, it might be the guy who was mailing the anthrax. He agreed. If this guy was an amateur — and remember, at the time, everyone thought al-Qaeda operatives were responsible — and wasn't doing it in a laboratory somewhere (which was unlikely), he would absolutely need a glovebox.

I called a friend who worked for the FBI in Washington and told him the story. He checked with his superiors and they suggested I call the FBI's Boston office, which is close to where I live.

With my neighbor's OK, I did this — and that's when things started to go wrong.

First of all, it took the FBI almost two weeks to get back to me. Again, remember that the news was full of how hard the FBI was working to catch this guy, which, knowing what I know now, had to be bullshit.

When an FBI agent finally called, I told him the story, explained what a glovebox was and that there were only five companies in the country that made them — two of which were in the town I lived in, and one of which was owned by my neighbor.

It took me a while to explain it all to him. At one point, he said the FBI had already checked this out, but I told him no one had ever contacted my neighbor's company. The agent took notes, I guess, and said he'd get back to me. He also wanted to talk to my neighbor.

My neighbor called him a few days later and essentially regurgitated what I had told the agent earlier. The agent said he'd get back to us.

Another two weeks went by. One night my phone rang. It was the FBI. A different agent. He started the conversation with: "I understand you know who the anthrax killer is."

I told him, no — I just had a theory on how the guy might be doing it, and that all the FBI had to do was check the records of these glovebox companies and see if anyone unusual had bought one lately. (BTW, gloveboxes aren't cheap. They cost about $30,000 each.)

The agent took my information — again — and then asked to speak with my neighbor, again. By this time we were getting PO'd that these guys were so disorganized. To watch the news — especially that propaganda operation Fox News — you would have thought the FBI was throwing every resource they had into this. Yet to us, they seemed bumbling and very disconnected.

My neighbor talked to them again, reluctantly by this time, and eventually, some agents arrived at the two glovebox companies in our town and went over their recent sales records. They spent no more than an hour in each place — not exactly Sherlock Holmes-stuff — and left.

By this time, my neighbor and I were sorry we ever got involved. When the FBI's visit to his company was reported in the local paper, it just made the whole situation worse because the impression was the company had been lax in who they sold their gloveboxes to — certainly not the case.

Bottom line: It took the FBI nearly two months to act on this, something that should have taken a day at the most.

So much for trying to help out.

Failing in Space

There's a theory that extraterrestrials have tried to interfere with humanity's access to outer space. But as the following examples show, most failures in the heavens can be blamed not on ETs, but on dumb human mistakes made right here on Earth.

The Challenger Disaster

Launched on January 28, 1986, in sub-freezing temperatures so President Reagan could mention it in his State of the Union speech that night, the space shuttle blew up 73 seconds into its flight due to a faulty rocket seal that had been adversely affected by the cold weather.

The accident killed all on board, including Christa McAuliffe, who had been selected to be the first teacher in space.

Apollo 13

In April 1970, an exposed wire and a malfunctioning fan caused half of Apollo 13's lunar vehicle to blow apart on its way to the moon.

Fortunately, NASA controllers were able to talk the three astronauts safely back to Earth.

The Columbia Accident

Unbeknownst to NASA, when the space shuttle Columbia was launched on January 16, 2003, a piece of insulating foam struck its wing. It did enough damage to cause the shuttle to burn up on re-entry two weeks later, killing all aboard.

The Genesis Probe

Launched in August 2001 on a mission to gather solar particles, Genesis crashed in the Utah desert three years later after its improperly packed parachute failed to open on re-entry.

SBIRS

SBIRS, the Space-Based Infrared System, was already plagued by $10 *billion* in cost overruns when the first of its several highly classified spy satellites lasted exactly seven seconds in space before going dead — causing one defense official to label it "a useless ice cube."

The Mars Polar Lander

This multimillion-dollar NASA probe was lost in December 1999 on its way to Mars after it was discovered that half the spacecraft had been built using Standard English measurements and the other half using the metric system.

The NOAA-19 Crash

On September 6, 2003, engineers working for Lockheed-Martin forgot to bolt down this multimillion-dollar climate research satellite before moving it, sending it crashing to the floor.

The Iran Monkey Launch

On September 12, 2011, Iran's Kavoshgar-5 rocket, carrying a live Rhesus monkey, mysteriously blew up on launch. It instantly killed its simian passenger and scuttled Iran's hopes of landing humans on the moon sometime within the next 500 years.

Phobos-Grunt

Designed to retrieve a sample of the Martian moon Phobos, this Russian space probe failed in orbit on January 15, 2012, sending 15 tons of highly toxic remains plunging back to Earth.

George Bush's Mission to Mars

Somehow believing it would be easier for astronauts to get to Mars by stopping on the moon first, on January 14, 2004, Dubya proposed just such a lunar layover in a $120 billion program that never got off the ground.

The WIRE Satellite

"Premature ejection" was determined to be the cause of failure of NASA's $73 million Wide Field Infrared Explorer (WIRE) satellite, designed to study distant galaxies. The cover for the satellite's elongated space telescope ejected too soon after launch on November 10, 1999, causing overheating and rapid deflation, rendering it useless.

The Alcantara Explosion

When Brazil's Alcantara VLS-1 rocket blew up on its launch pad in August 2003, it destroyed the two satellites onboard and killed 21 people, including many of Brazil's top rocket scientists — setting the country's space program back years.

The Glory Hole

NASA's $424 million Glory atmospheric research satellite was declared a total loss on March 4, 2011, after the nose cone on its Taurus booster rocket failed to separate on launch. On February 4, 2009, NASA's $273 million Orbiting Carbon Observatory was also deemed a failure when it suffered a similar nose-cone mishap. Combined loss to U.S. taxpayers: $697 million.

The Space Hobo

Launched on October 27, 2010, the Eutelsat W3B satellite was declared a total loss less than 24 hours later due to a catastrophic leak in its propulsion system. Because ground controllers are unable to steer it, the satellite will spend the next 25 years drifting aimlessly in space.

The Space Brie Disaster

France's only attempt to put a man on the moon ended in failure when its bullet-shaped space capsule failed to make a soft landing on the lunar surface.

NASA Conspiracies

But for all the accomplishments this government agency can legitimately lay claim to — lunar exploration, landing vehicles on Mars, exploring the solar system —it cannot escape being suspect in some of the most monumental conspiracy theories ever.

Here are fifteen of them:

1. Did NASA fake the moon landings?

This long-running conspiracy theory claims NASA didn't have adequate technology in 1969 to reach the moon, so the agency fabricated the landings by secretly filming them in a movie studio.

Conspiracists seem to have just one piece of evidence: No stars can be seen in any of the photographs or videos shot during the lunar landings.

NASA claims the moon's surface is so reflective that it washed out any stars that may have been caught on film.

You decide.

2. Does NASA have photos of alien structures on the moon?

Several conspiracy-themed books claim there are extensive alien ruins on the dark side of the moon and that NASA has been keeping them secret for years.

These ruins are said to include structures several miles high. Conspiracists say that NASA astronauts took pictures of the ruins during trips to the moon — which means that, to believe this theory, you cannot believe the moon landings were faked in the first place.

3. Rocket to nowhere

As mentioned earlier, in January 2004, President George W. Bush proposed a bold mission for NASA: Build a new kind of spaceship, use it to take astronauts back to the moon, and then carry them on to Mars.

NASA immediately embraced the $120 billion plan. But just five years later, the Bush initiative was in ruins.

In 2009, a committee charged with looking into the plan called it "the wrong destination with the wrong rocket." Citing wildly optimistic goals and a near complete lack of funding, NASA scrapped the whole idea — but not before spending millions on its "rocket to nowhere."

4. Is NASA trying to establish a New World Order?

This way-out theory started in 1994, when Canadian author Serge Monast claimed he'd uncovered a massive conspiracy by NASA to enslave the world's population.

Project Blue Beam, Monast said, was a NASA plan to put on what he called the "Big Space Show in the Sky" in which a holographic projection of God would appear in the heavens and speak to everyone on Earth, misleading them into accepting the Antichrist as their leader.

Monast believed clues to fantastic event could be found in films such as *Independence Day* and *Jurassic Park.*

Monast died of a heart attack in 1996 after spending a night in jail on a domestic charge, leading many of his followers to claim he was murdered by NASA assassins for knowing too much.

5. Is NASA lying about the "Face on Mars"?

In July 1976, NASA's Viking spacecraft took a picture of a mysterious formation on the surface of Mars.

The photo seemed to show a huge face, leading many to suggest it was proof that an alien civilization once inhabited the Red Planet.

But NASA claimed the "face" was just a set of crumbling hills whose shadows created the illusion of an intelligently designed monument.

Although Mars's surface has been photographed thousands of times since, many conspiracy theorists are still convinced that NASA is lying and that the face is real.

6. Is NASA covering up how the Challenger astronauts died?

On January 28, 1986, the space shuttle Challenger blew up shortly after takeoff from Cape Canaveral.

After millions watching on TV saw the spacecraft disintegrate in a huge explosion, NASA suggested the Challenger's crew, including teacher Christa McAuliffe, all died instantly.

Yet conspiracy theorists have long claimed that NASA possesses a secret tape recording, made moments after the explosion, of weeping, panicked cries and astronauts speaking final messages to their families.

NASA has gone to court in attempts to keep secret photographs and other evidence it has pertaining to the Challenger explosion, fueling the conspiracy fire.

7. Does NASA really know what caused the Columbia disaster?

On February 1, 2003, the shuttle Columbia burned up on re-entry to Earth, killing its seven-person crew, including Israeli astronaut Ilan Ramon.

Ramon was a former Israeli Air Force pilot who took part in the 1981 bombing of an Iraqi nuclear reactor near Baghdad.

Some conspiracy theorists claim that, for revenge, Iraqi dictator Saddam Hussein built a secret laser weapon that was fired at Columbia as it flew over the Middle East on its final orbit, causing it to disintegrate in the upper atmosphere.

NASA, however, has stuck to its story that the shuttle was struck during takeoff by a loose piece of foam insulation, and that this damage caused it to break apart on re-entry.

8. Does NASA have a secret space program?

Many within the conspiracy community believe that NASA's reputation for fumbling and bumbling is simply a cover for an enormous secret space program.

They insist the space agency has hundreds of manned spacecraft capable of reaching all the planets in the solar system.

Proponents of this theory point to the claim that NASA has photographs of hundreds of "unknown space-craft" in Earth's orbit but refuses to release them to the public.

The conspiracy buffs say the photos either depict UFOs or vehicles belonging to this hidden space program that, for unexplained reasons, NASA craves to keep secret.

9. Did NASA allow extraterrestrials to ride on the space shuttle?

In 2008, a former NASA employee claimed that while watching a video transmission at Mission Control years before, he'd seen an alien aboard a space shuttle while it was in orbit.

The ex-NASA employee said the creature was eight feet tall and was standing upright in the shuttle cargo bay having a conversation with two tethered shuttle astronauts while an alien spacecraft flew nearby.

While NASA would probably never even address such claims — and the employee has long since been fired from the space agency — the story's proponents point out that the shuttle flight in question had been a top-secret mission for the U.S. Defense Department.

10. Is NASA planning a race of Super Soldiers?

In 2010, NASA announced it had discovered a new microbe in a salt lake in California that was unlike anything ever found on Earth.

Because this microbe could exist in an extremely harsh environment, the space agency said the discovery could increase the chances of finding life in outer space.

But conspiracy theorists claim the new microbe is actually extraterrestrial in origin, having arrived on Earth thousands of years ago.

They suspect NASA's real motive in revealing the new microbe is to raise an army of super soldiers that would not need oxygen to breathe, allowing them to survive underwater or in the airless reaches of space.

11. Trouble with Hubble, Part 1

For years, NASA claimed that the Hubble Space Telescope, known for taking fantastic pictures of objects light-years from Earth, could not take photographs of the moon because of its high reflectivity and the space telescope's resolution limitations.

Then, in April 1999, NASA revealed that it had indeed taken photos of the moon with the Hubble, but that their resolution was too large to show things like the Apollo landing sites, which conspiracy theorists say don't exist.

Why would NASA mislead people about its ability to photograph the moon with the Hubble?

12. Trouble with Hubble, Part 2

Is the Hubble telescope really just a spy satellite?

Conspiracy theorists claim that, far from being a unique deep-space telescope, Hubble is actually a spy satellite built from secret U.S. military designs.

A story published in May 2009 said that before the Hubble was launched, its outer casing was accidentally cracked, threatening the future of the multibillion dollar-satellite. At the last minute, the Defense Department secretly gave NASA a casing of its own, leading conspiracy buffs to ask why the U.S. military would have such a casing.

13. We Thought You Already Knew

On September 19, 2016, a website called Disclose.tv reported that a highly placed NASA official had admitted the space agency had had contact with extraterrestrials, that ETs were running mining operations on the far side of the moon, and that they helped build the pyramids in Egypt thousands of years ago.

Asked why NASA was making these startling admissions now, the website said the space agency never formally announced its findings because it assumed everyone was already aware of them.

It turns out Disclose.tv was unwittingly duped. The source for its article was a satirical website called Waterford Whispers, a sort of Irish version of The Onion, which in the past has reported other items mistaken as real news — including one claiming that the pope had asked Harry Potter author J.K. Rowling to rewrite the Bible.

14. Is NASA covering up sex in space?

Have NASA astronauts had sex in space?

The official word from the agency is "no," even though there is nothing in NASA's rulebook that specifically prohibits celestial relations.

But even though rumors persist that NASA carried out secret sex experiments in space when the shuttle was still flying, information vital for two-year round-trip flights to Mars, one astronaut said we would have known if anyone had engaged in cosmic coitus.

"Guys are guys," shuttle astronaut Leroy Chiao was quoted as saying. "If a guy had sex in space, he would not be able to not brag about it."

15. <u>Did the Nazis help NASA land on the moon?</u>

After World War II, dozens of Nazi scientists were allowed into the United States under a secret program called Operation Paperclip.

Even though many of these scientists had helped Hitler create weapons that killed thousands during the war, they had their records wiped clean and were put to work on the newborn U.S. space program, creating the foundation of NASA.

One of the scientists, Werner Von Braun, rose to the top of the NASA hierarchy, and it was his rocket design that got astronauts to the moon.

So, in this case, the conspiracy theory is true.

Weird Celebrity Deaths

Sometimes the famous die gloriously.
Sometimes they don't.

General George Patton

Patton's army killed nearly a million Germans in World War II — but who killed Patton?

Soon after suggesting Nazi soldiers could help the U.S. attack then-ally Russia, the outspoken war hero was involved in a mysterious car accident near Mannheim, Germany, suffering injuries that killed him three weeks later.

Pope John Paul I

There's no shortage of conspiracy theories concerning the demise of this pontiff, who lasted barely a month.

Found dead in his bed by a nun, was he murdered to thwart a probe of the Vatican Bank? Was he assassinated by the KGB for his pledge to fight communism?

Or had he just opened the mysterious Third Secret of Fatima and was literally shocked to death by what he'd read?

Whitney Houston

The onetime superstar died in her Beverly Hilton suite's bathtub on February 11, 2012.

The preliminary cause of death was ruled accidental drowning, complicated by heart disease and cocaine use. Yet one conspiracy theory claims Houston was actually murdered by a cult of Satan worshipers inside the music industry.

The theory suggests Houston made a pledge to the devil just before she became a worldwide sensation, that her ex-husband Bobby Brown was selected by the Satanists to be her "mind manipulator," and that once she was used up, she was sacrificed for the good of the cult.

If so, where was her bodyguard when she needed him?

Vincent Van Gogh

No doubt Vincent Van Gogh was a tortured artist, but was he also a murder victim?

Most believe that on July 27, 1890, the 37-year-old painter shot himself while standing in a wheat field about a mile from his home near Paris. Though the bullet missed his vital organs, Van Gogh died 30 hours later from an infection caused by the gunshot's wound.

But some recent research suggests Van Gogh may have been shot by a pair of local youths who had been bullying him. Two clues: The gun Van Gogh supposedly used to shoot himself was never found, and when police asked him shortly before he died if he had tried to kill himself, Van Gogh replied: "I believe so," but then strangely requested that no one else be accused of the crime.

Sonny Bono

Best known for being Cher's first husband, singer Sonny Bono managed to get elected to the U.S. Congress in 1995, only to die in January 1998 after skiing into a tree near Lake Tahoe.

Though his death was ruled an accident, rumors persist that, having been tipped off that high-ranking U.S. military personnel were illegally selling weapons and drugs in Central America, Bono was murdered to keep him quiet about the allegations.

AKA Nebkheperure

He had curvature of the spine, a bizarre elongated head, a cleft palate, and a hideous overbite. He also suffered from mental retardation and a host of other genetic defects as a result of his incestuous birth. Yet he managed to rule Egypt as a child of ten and become the best-known pharaoh of today.

His name was King Tut. But how did he die? Many believe he was murdered by hangers-on, jealous that a boy was running the vast Egyptian empire. Other theories include malaria, sickle cell anemia, and accidental poisoning.

But after doing a CAT-scan of his mummy, scientists now believe Tut died from a simple broken leg that became infected. They theorize that the injury was caused when he accidently fell off his chariot.

Joseph P. Kennedy Jr.

President John F. Kennedy's older brother was a Navy pilot during World War II. Prodded by JFK's well-publicized PT-109 heroics in the Pacific, brother Joe volunteered to fly an explosives-laden airplane toward Nazi territory, bailing out only once it was set to crash into an enemy target.

But something went wrong and the airplane blew up prematurely, instantly killing Kennedy and his copilot.

Laura Bush's Boyfriend

One fall day in 1963, the future first lady ran a stop sign and hit another car, killing the occupant.

The dead man happened to be her ex-boyfriend, who'd recently dumped her to date one of her best friends. Though conspiracy theories claiming Laura did it on purpose seem farfetched, parts of the accident report were obscured, and for some reason, police at the scene failed to give her a sobriety test.

William Henry Harrison

The ninth president of the United States spent much of his cold and rainy Inauguration Day outside without a coat.

As a result, he developed pneumonia. Harrison's physicians treated him with everything from castor oil to opium and even tried leeches, but nothing worked.

Harrison died on April 4, 1841, just thirty-three days after taking office.

Warren G. Harding

The 29th president died in a San Francisco hotel room on August 2, 1923 — but of what?

Harding had two mistresses, making his wife insanely jealous. His administration was corrupt and under investigation. He'd had several nervous breakdowns in his earlier days, plus he'd eaten some bad crab on a recent trip to Alaska.

So, was it a heart attack, a stroke, food poisoning, or maybe even murder? His doctors could never agree.

Zachary Taylor

After spending a sweltering July day watching a groundbreaking ceremony for the Washington Monument, the 12th president of the United States tried to cool off by drinking lots of cold milk and eating lots of cherries. Big mistake.

He contracted a severe digestive ailment and died on July 9, 1850. Official cause of death: "bilious diarrhea."

King Adolf Frederick

This Swedish monarch died in 1771 after consuming immense quantities of lobster, caviar, sauerkraut, cabbage soup, smoked herring, champagne, and more than a dozen servings of dessert — all in one meal.

No surprise, in Sweden, Frederick is known as *Konung som åt sig till döden"* — the "King Who Ate Himself to Death."

Alexander 1

This Greek king was taking his dog for a walk in his Royal Gardens one day in 1920 when the dog was attacked by a monkey.

Attempting to save his pet, the king was severely bitten by the simian and its mate.

His wounds became septic, and Alexander was dead three weeks later.

Clement Vallandigham

While defending a client against a murder charge, this Civil War-era congressman argued that the victim could have killed himself with his own pistol.

To demonstrate his point, Vallandigham pulled out a loaded gun and accidently shot himself in the leg, severing a major artery.

He died instantly.

Bob Crane

Best known for portraying the Nazi-baiting POW officer in the long-running TV series "Hogan's Heroes," actor Bob Crane had a decidedly kinky side to his personal life. Having access to early versions of handheld video cameras, Crane recorded hundreds of sexual encounters with a bevy of women.

The fun and games came to a grisly end, though, on June 28, 1978, when Crane was found savagely beaten to death in an Arizona hotel room. Suspicion immediately fell on his sexcapades cameraman, a friend named John Carpenter, but Carpenter was later found not guilty of Crane's killing.

But whoever did it wanted to send a very personal message, as police reported that the killer ejaculated on Crane's body after murdering him.

Bon Scott

Death by vomit? Heroin? Car exhaust? Or just the cold? Take your pick when it comes to the untimely demise of AC/DC lead singer Bon Scott.

On February 19, 1980, the Aussie front man was seen drinking heavily at a London bar. A friend offered to let him sleep it off at his house, but Scott was too drunk to move when they arrived and remained in the car overnight. Scott's friend found him dead the next day.

While the authorities said Scott choked on his own vomit, rumors persist that he succumbed to a heroin overdose or froze to death, or even that someone manipulated the car's exhaust pipe, poisoning him.

In any case, AC/DC soon recruited a new singer and went on to record "Back in Black," the third bestselling rock album in history.

Amy Winehouse

Few people were shocked when, on July 23, 2011, singer Amy Winehouse died at age 27.

The singer was known for sloppy performances, over-indulging in intoxicants, and embarrassing incidents with the paparazzi. Her family initially theorized that she died because she'd given up alcohol *too quickly* — ignoring her doctors' advice to get off the booze gradually.

In reality, coroners found immense quantities of alcohol in her system at the time of death, more than five times the legal limit. In other words, Amy Winehouse drank herself to death.

David Carradine

From grasshopper to "gasper"?

Best known for his role in the early 1970s TV series "Kung Fu," actor David Carradine met a strange demise in a Bangkok hotel room on June 3, 2009.

Wearing fishnet stockings and a woman's wig, the 73-year-old star was found hanging in a closet with a rope tied around his neck, wrist, and genitalia.

While two of his ex-wives confirmed Carradine was a "gasper" — someone who engages in near-asphyxiation as a means of sexual arousal — a Carradine family lawyer suggested the actor might have been murdered, the result of his "investigation of martial arts secret societies." The same theory surfaced in the strange death of another martial arts star, the great Bruce Lee, 36 years before.

David Austin

Few people are cut out to be survivalists, and to fail at it usually means death. That seems to have been the case with David Austin, 29, from Derby, England.

Austin set off in November 2011 determined to survive the harsh winter of the Scottish Highlands, even though friends and family repeatedly warned him he wasn't qualified to endure the extreme elements. Even expert survivalists say three days is the limit for living in the rugged highlands.

Without a means to keep sufficiently warm or to catch and eat wildlife for nourishment, Austin was found dead on December 31 in a small cabin in one of the most inhospitable places in the British Isles, literally out in the middle of nowhere.

James Forrestal

Locked up for psychiatric problems at the National Naval Medical Center in Bethesda Maryland, on May 22, 1949, Harry Truman's secretary of defense either fell or jumped from a sixteenth-story window, ending it all.

What drove Forrestal mad? Was it cutthroat Washington politics? Or his claim that "foreign agents" were following him? Or was it evidence he'd seen proving the existence of UFOs?

All three rumors persist to this day.

Jack Wheeler

A respected Pentagon official, Wheeler went missing in late 2010 only to show up on security cameras wandering around Wilmington, Delaware, wearing only one shoe and dressed in unfamiliar clothes.

He was later found in a landfill, dead of blunt-force trauma.

Senator Charles Percy's daughter

On September 18, 1966, someone broke into the Chicago-area home of presidential-hopeful Senator Charles Percy and murdered his 21-year-old daughter as she slept.

Was it a random act or was someone sending Percy a message? Either way, he never ran for president — and his daughter's murder remains unsolved.

Ron Brown

Bill Clinton's commerce secretary raised so much money for Bubba's presidential campaign that he became the target of a government investigation.

A major embarrassment for the Clinton White House was averted, though, when Brown's plane mysteriously crashed into a mountain in Bosnia, killing him and everyone else on board.

Vince Foster

This friend of the Clintons left his White House office one day in July 1993, drove to a nearby park, and shot himself.

Although a suicide note was found, conspiracy theories persist that Foster was murdered to keep him quiet about a pending White House scandal or an affair with Hillary.

Jon-Erik Hexum

In one of the weirdest celebrity deaths ever, actor Jon-Erik Hexum was killed by a wad of paper.

The star of the '80s TV show "Cover Up," Hexum was on the set one day, pretending to play Russian roulette with a handgun used in an earlier scene. The pistol had been loaded with blanks, wadded-up pieces of paper used instead of real bullets. Yet blanks can still be dangerous if fired at close range.

Either thinking it was empty or that its blank cartridges would not hurt him, Hexum put the gun to his head and pulled the trigger. The force of the paper wad hitting his temple was enough to shatter his skull and send bone fragments into his brain. He died six days later.

Brandon Lee

In an eerily similar tragedy, Brandon Lee, son of actor Bruce Lee, was killed by a prop gun while shooting the movie "The Crow."

A pistol loaded with real bullets had been used in a prior scene. When the same gun was used to film Lee's death scene, no one realized one real bullet was still stuck in the gun's barrel. When a blank cartridge was fired, it provided enough force to push the real bullet out of the barrel and into Lee's abdomen, killing him.

Although conspiracy buffs blame the same martial arts secret societies that supposedly killed his father, this weird celebrity death appears to have been purely accidental.

Ray Combs

Best known for hosting the TV game show "Family Feud" in the '90s, Ray Combs was plagued by personal demons in the last years of his life.

In 1994, a car accident nearly paralyzed him, leaving him in constant pain. Business problems followed, his house was repossessed, and then he and his wife split.

Combs attempted suicide twice after that, by leaping from a moving car and by banging his head against the wall of his home. Committed to a psychiatric ward in June 1996, he hanged himself in his hospital room closet by wrapping his bedsheet around a bar that was designed to break away on just such occasions, but didn't.

Vic Morrow

Death by helicopter.

In one of the grislier celebrity deaths, Vic Morrow, actor and father of actress Jennifer Jason Leigh, was killed when a helicopter being used to shoot a scene for the film "Twilight Zone: The Movie" crashed on top of him and two child actors.

Struck by the whirring helicopter blades, Morrow was decapitated.

Though director John Landis and producer Steven Spielberg were charged with involuntary manslaughter in the incident, those charges were later dropped.

Sal Mineo

Sal Mineo was one of the top actors in Hollywood in the 1950s.

Nominated twice for an Academy Award, he co-starred with James Dean in "Rebel Without a Cause." And even though Mineo had been reduced to playing a chimpanzee in "Escape from the Planet of the Apes" in 1971, his career was starting to turn around in 1976 when he was stabbed to death in a West Hollywood alley by a pizza deliveryman.

While it was well known that Mineo liked sado-masochistic sex, police said his murder was simply a robbery gone wrong. Yet his strange death only added fuel to the myth that "Rebel Without a Cause" was cursed.

James Dean

James Dean might have been the coolest actor who ever lived, but his status of celebrity myth was ensured by his death on September 30, 1955.

Always the thrill-seeker, Dean had purchased a Porsche 550 racecar. While driving it to a race in Salinas, California, and shortly after receiving a speeding ticket, Dean collided head-on with a car that had crossed into his lane, killing him.

Dean had starred in only three movies before he died; his most famous, "Rebel Without a Cause," came out a month after his death and was a huge hit. Yet with the untimely deaths of his "Rebel" co-stars Natalie Wood (bizarre drowning in 1981) and Sal Mineo (gruesomely murdered in 1976), many wonder if that iconic movie is truly cursed.

Monster Mania!

Agogwe

Half-man, half-monkey, the Agogwe are said to inhabit the forests of East Africa. Only about four feet tall, they have rust-colored hair covering most of their bodies. Though they walk upright and display many human characteristics, these strange creatures are most often spotted feeding alongside baboons.

Blood Beast of Bladenboro

In the winter of 1953, something was killing dogs in Bladenboro, North Carolina, and sucking the blood from their bodies. Witnesses described the mystery creature as cat-like, six feet long and covered with black fur. It killed at least a half-dozen canines, all of them found with their heads crushed, their tongues ripped out, and their bodies drained of blood.

Coelacanth

This prehistoric fish was assumed extinct about 65 million years ago. That's why scientists were shocked in December 1938, when a five-foot-long, 125-pound Coelacanth was caught off the coast of South Africa.

Dingonek

Said to dwell in the rivers of West Africa, this hideous creature has a large, square head, reptile-like claws, and two curved tusks that give it the nickname "The Jungle Walrus." The Dingonek is rumored to grow up to twenty feet long, and its bony tail contains a sharpened appendage filled with deadly poison.

Ebu Gogo

Also called "real Hobbits," this race of miniature humans — first seen by Portuguese sea traders in the 17th century — are said to still inhabit the Indonesia island of Flores. Just three feet tall, with hairy bodies and flat noses, the Ebu Gogo have their own language, are adept jungle dwellers, but are extremely shy. Similar creatures called the Orang Pendek are rumored to live on the nearby island of Sumatra.

Fear Liath Mor

This creature, extremely tall, with short gray hair and an "inhuman" face, inhabits the highest peaks of the Scottish Highlands. Sightings of the Fear Liath Mor go back to the 13th century. While only a few mountain climbers have seen the monster in recent years, many others report suddenly being overwhelmed by feelings of panic and fear while climbing in the area.

Globsters

This term describes mysterious globs of flesh and bone that occasionally wash up on the world's beaches, thought by many to be the remains of sea serpents. Some scientists claim globsters are actually the decomposed bodies of giant octopuses, though no one knows for sure.

Honey Island Swamp Monster

Louisiana's Honey Island Swamp is said to be home to this ape-like creature that leaves giant, three-toed footprints wherever it goes. Often compared to Bigfoot, the beast achieved notoriety in the 1970s when it was caught on film by the TV show "In Search Of ..."

Igopogo

Said to be more than twenty feet long, weighing several hundred pounds and covered in gray fur, this water monster calls Ontario's Lake Simcoe its home. While descriptions vary, most witnesses say Igopogo resembles a gigantic seal with a strange, dog-like head.

J'Ba Fofi

Also known as the Congolese Giant Spider, these creatures grow in excess of five feet and weave webs 15 feet across. Black, with tarantula-like fur and, some say, glowing eyes, the monstrous arachnids use their gigantic webs to trap birds, rodents, and even baby antelopes, entangling and then encasing their bodies to be devoured later.

Kasai Rex

Another inhabitant of the deep Congo, the Kasai Rex is a giant lizard said to grow to 40 feet or more. Seen mostly by workers on isolated jungle plantations, the creature has been described as a "T-Rex with fins on its back," giving it a distinct dragon-like appearance.

Lake Worth Monster

In July 1969, the small city of Lake Worth, Texas, was terrorized by a creature described as half-man, half-goat. Numerous witnesses spotted the beast near water and lurking along isolated country roads. One man reported it jumped onto his car from a tree, causing an 18-inch dent in the hood. Police investigated, but the Lake Worth Monster disappeared soon afterward.

Man-Eating Tree of Madagascar

As reported by an Australian newspaper in 1881, this carnivorous tree was actually a gigantic Venus flytrap to which local tribes would sacrifice females in return for blessings from the spirits. One witness wrote of seeing a victim first embraced by the tree's tentacles and then squeezed to death, after which her bodily fluids were sucked out, leaving little more than skin and bones.

Nain Rouge

French for "Red Dwarf," this creature haunts the suburbs of Detroit. Witnesses say it looks like a small child with red-and-black fur, glowing eyes, and protruding, rotting teeth. Two people who saw it in 1996 claimed it made a cawing sound like a crow. Cryptozoologists say that when the creature makes an appearance, some kind of tragedy usually follows.

Olgoi-Khorkhoi

Also known as the Mongolian Death Worm, this creature grows up to six feet with a thick body that's colored blood red. Greatly feared among the native Mongolian people, the worm can kill either by spraying its victims with a lethal poison or by transmitting a high-voltage charge that electrocutes them.

Piasa

With a name that means "giant bird that devours man," this winged monster was first spotted in the 1700s in present-day Illinois. Larger than a cow, with horns like a deer, the eyes of a mountain cat, and a face like a man, it's said to be capable of carrying off a full-grown deer.

However, as the name indicates, its favorite meal is human flesh.

Q-Beast

Taking a dark turn on the Goldilocks story, this "land octopus" is said to haunt the small island of Intuba off the Pacific coast of Panama. Witnesses say the monster will enter an empty home, eat any food it can find, and then devour the residents when they return.

Ratosaurus

Two of these heretofore mythical rodents have been found recently, one living in a volcano in New Guinea, the other under a sporting goods store in the Bronx. Said to be almost three feet long and weighing nearly ten pounds, the giant Bronx specimen was described as "not your average subway rat."

Skunk Ape

This Bigfoot-like creature is said to inhabit Florida's vast Everglades. Standing eight feet tall and weighing at least 300 pounds, it emits an odor that's a nauseating mix of skunk, rotten eggs, and cow droppings.

Tatzelwurm

This lizard-like creature has been spotted in the Swiss Alps for centuries. It can grow up to seven feet long and is highly poisonous. Some scientists think the Tatzelwurm is related to the equally venomous Gila monster of the American Southwest.

Ucu

More than ten feet tall and covered with long, dark hair, this South American monster is said to possess many humanlike features. Ucus are usually spotted high in the Andes Mountains and are known to scream at livestock, frightening them to death. Ucus also have reportedly trapped people and held them captive. One explorer says that if you urinate on an Ucu, it will immediately let you go.

Vampire Bird

Rumored to live only in the Galapagos Islands, this innocent looking finch has developed a taste for other birds' blood over the centuries. Attacking its prey by incessantly pecking at their bodies until the skin is broken, the winged vampire will suck its host's blood for however long it takes to be satiated.

Wendigo

This man-like beast is frequently sighted in the forests of northern Minnesota. Said to have a skeletal, almost corpse-like body covered by sickly gray skin, it emits a foul odor similar to a decomposing carcass. Native American lore says Wendigos have a voracious appetite for human flesh and lurk in the forests especially during the winter, looking for prey.

Xing-Xing

Sightings of this beast are frequent in southern China. Standing upright like a man, it has long arms and legs and is covered with orange hair. Some scientists believe the animal is a prehistoric version of the orangutan that somehow survived the ages.

Yell Hound

This enormous, sometimes headless dog is said to roam the outskirts of Devon, England. Described as being the size of a cow, it stalks the woods and backroads at night, making horrible wailing noises. Some speculate the Yell Hound served as inspiration for the ghost dog in the Sherlock Holmes adventure "Hound of the Baskervilles."

Zeuglodons

These prehistoric whales are believed to have gone extinct 30 million years ago. But if they're still around today, they might explain the many modern reports of sea serpents and lake monsters. Looking nothing like today's whales, Zeuglodons were long and serpentine and may have crawled overland to spawn in secluded lakes.

My Beef With Spielberg

Steven Spielberg is a very successful movie director — but that doesn't mean he's a great one.

This is probably my Emerson College film school education talking, but he's made some pretty bad movies, at least as I remember them.

What's tough for me is that lots of people think the Spielberg movies I think are bad, are great.

Jurassic Park

It only takes one scene to ruin a movie. In this film it's the bizarre ice cream scene that ends the second act. Laura Dern's two movie kids are lost out in the park with hundreds of ravenous meat-eating dinosaurs ready to tear them apart. Richard Attenborough is the guy who built the park and created those monsters.

Night has fallen, and after basically calling off the search for her children until morning, mother and mad scientist are holed up in his jungle mansion.

So what do they do?

They sit at a table, eat ice cream … and talk about their day.

A.I.

Maybe sometime in the far-flung future the letters "AI" will translate into "what a fucking mess." If it happens, it will be because of this Spielberg clam.

Spielberg took an unfinished script by movie-god Stanley Kubrick, finished it, and filmed it after Kubrick died.

A.I. tells the story of David, a childlike android uniquely programmed with the ability to love. Isn't that precious? He wanders around a post-apocalyptic world basically retracing the steps of the Pinocchio story. And for a lot of the film, his one and only friend is his teddy bear.

But then he goes to this bad-trip carnival, loses his toy, and has a major meltdown. Not good for an android. Yet as this sequence is ending, David is shown walking out of the creepy fairgrounds — clutching his Teddy! How'd he get him back? We have no idea. No explanation is ever given.

War of the Worlds

This is probably Spielberg's least whimsical film, which is saying a lot. It gets off to rocky start when the lead character, played by Tom Cruise, is first shown operating one of those huge cargo-container cranes on the Brooklyn docks and then going home to his shabby house in shabby Bayonne, New Jersey. Really? Do you have any idea how much those crane operators make?

Anyway, the action and special effects are pretty good as the Martians attack and divorcee Tom struggles against everything they can throw at him to get his kids up to Boston, where their mother is. No small feat, as the invaders are absolutely ruthless, immune to our weapons, and have a taste for human flesh, snatching up innocents, eating them alive, and expunging a bloody goo afterward.

But again, there's that one bad scene and in this movie, it comes at the end. Make no mistake; the world as we know it is destroyed. The Martians' murderous rampage is stopped only because earthly bacteria do them in. The second to last sequence shows a long shot of Boston, flattened and in flames. Seeing that, I remember thinking: Hey, I can see my old house from here.

But for some reason, the devastation missed the very tony Beantown neighborhood — actually, it looks a little more Cambridge-y — where Tom's ex has been staying with her parents.

Tom shows up to deliver their daughter to her. (His older, sullen son becomes lost halfway through the film and is assumed dead, but somehow pulled through and made it to the Hub on his own.) Tom's ex comes out of her parents' townhouse dressed as if she'd been doing little more than having a cup of coffee and mulling over *The Times* crossword puzzle.

The most damage you can see is that the street has maybe twice as many leaves on it as would seem normal. There's no human mulch, no dead aliens, no icky distractions. Tom has succeeded in his mission and heads off into the sunset.

In film school this kind of weepy scene is known as "handkerchiefing" (aka the Moment of Shit), that tearjerking ending to your final project that guarantees you at least a B. But Spielberg graduated film school in 1968 — and *War of the Worlds* was made in 2005.

Didn't he learn anything else along the way?

Saving Private Ryan

The beginning is brilliant film-making. No big-time movie recreates the horrors of war better than the opening sequence showing the D-Day landings. When I saw it, I thought it should be mandatory viewing for all high school seniors in case they're considering joining the military. Not that they shouldn't serve the country, but it's wise to get some idea what you might be getting into.

Anyway, an order from Washington (sent practically by FDR himself) reaches the Normandy beachhead. It concerns Private James Ryan, a paratrooper just dropped behind enemy lines. Ryan has three brothers, and they've all been killed in combat. Should he also get killed, it will be a huge public relations problem for the White House.

Lieutenant Tom Hanks and his squad are sent out to look for Private Ryan and bring him back alive. The squad ventures into enemy territory and commences a bloody journey that has a very bloody ending.

But let's think about this for a moment. The *President* wants you to find this guy, and you send out only eight soldiers? On foot?

What do you think all those tanks are for? Why wouldn't you send a dozen or more to do the job?

Raiders of the Lost Ark

Sheldon said it best:

Nothing the main characters do in this film — the fights, the rescues, the airplane, the submarine — has any effect on the outcome of the story. The Nazis steal the Ark of the Covenant, bring it to their lair, open it, and get melted down by the banshee-like spirits inside. Indy and his buds have nothing to do with it.

"There's a lack of connection there, Mr. Spielberg. That will be twenty-five points off your final grade."

Close Encounters of the Third Kind

According to a 1982 report in <u>The New York Times</u>, large quantities of illegal drugs were consumed during the making of this movie. The film's producer, Julia Phillips, once estimated she alone spent more than $1 million on a cocaine habit that started with the filming of *CE3.* That's a lot of blow, folks.

Spielberg has never been accused of being a coke head, and frankly he doesn't seem the type. But the star of this 1976 movie, Richard Dreyfus, has had highly-publicized run-ins with the substance, and I think that might be why he does such a sucky job in this movie. In any case, he's the absolute wrong person for the part.

To start off with, it's a weird script. Dreyfus encounters a couple of UFOs and then is compelled to create, in his dining room, a scale model of a specific but unusual mountain using anything he can get his hands on, including mashed potatoes. This eventually leads him, some government scientists, and the U.S. military to Devil's Tower, Wyoming, where an extraterrestrial spaceship lands and commences what we assume will be friendly relations.

Dreyfus walks through the film like he's in a different movie, a rom-com, perhaps. The gravity of the situation never shows on him. He acts doofy, scattered, and, hmmm, what's the word? Whimsical? And in almost every scene, he looks, well … a little duzzed up.

Again, the movie was made in 1976, but the special effects it required just weren't around yet. Early scenes in which actors and UFOs appear together look like they're edited with scotch tape. The flying saucers don't have the right proportion to the actors, and the actors are frequently looking in a different direction than they should be.

I'd read that most of the grand finale was filmed inside an aircraft hangar. It looks it. Hundreds of people, staring slightly upward and trying hard to look awe-struck while pretending to watch a huge UFO land. There's *lots* of that.

There are also lots of scenes of the military on the move. Trucks, Jeeps, secret-looking tractor-trailers rushing around to great choreography, but many times it's not really clear what they are doing or where they are going. The adult version of playing trucks.

But the *real* problem is that the movie doesn't tell a good story. Originally the main character was supposed to be a military officer who doesn't believe in UFOs suddenly having his life turned upside down. They should have gone with that one, and gotten anyone other than Dreyfus to play the lead.

Full disclosure: I wrote a large part of my grad school thesis on this movie, so I've seen it many, many times.

Watch anything that much and it will lose its luster. But I also remember being disappointed the very first time I saw it.

Remakes are a big deal these days. Spielberg should remake this movie.

E.T.

At the beginning of this film, little E.T. is chased by some Earthlings through some dark woods and, as a result, can't get back to his spaceship and is left behind by his friends.

Later on, after E.T. makes new friends with some Earth kids, he uses his extraterrestrial powers to fulfill every kid's dream of being able to fly if you just pedal your bike hard enough. It's the most famous scene in the movie, E.T. enabling this little group of kids on bikes to fly with him.

But if E.T. can fly — why didn't he fly away from the guys who were chasing him at the beginning?

Jaws

Released in 1975, this movie is responsible for the needless killing of thousands of sharks around the world, a savagery that has led to the collapse of a really fragile ecosystem and …

Only kidding. I never saw it.

14 Real Movie Monsters

1. King Kong

Possibly the most famous monster movie of all time, the original 1933 *King Kong* is the classic Beauty and the Beast story told in disguise.

The giant ape Kong falls in love with beautiful actress Ann Darrow and then pays the price by getting shot off the Empire State Building by fighter planes.

But was King Kong real? Scientists believe a creature of similar description roamed the Earth nine million years ago. It was called "Gigantopithecus blacki," and fossil records suggest this real monster stood more than ten feet tall and may have weighed close to a ton.

2. Godzilla

Making its screen debut in 1954, the giant prehistoric lizard named Godzilla went on to stomp Tokyo in twenty-eight films.

Incredibly the Kasai Rex, mentioned earlier as being a "T-Rex with fins on its back" and rumored to live in the deepest part of the Congo, matches the description of movie Godzilla almost perfectly.

3. Rodan

Released in 1956, this movie tells the tale of a huge flying monster similar to a prehistoric pterodactyl that lays waste to Tokyo.

As we will learn later, a creature of comparable description and with a similar-sounding name has been rumored to inhabit remote parts of New Guinea.

Called the Ropen, this flying dinosaur-like beast is seen only at night, can glow in the dark, and reportedly has a taste for dead humans.

4. Sharktopus

In this 2010 cult movie favorite, the U.S. Navy genetically engineers a creature that's half-shark and half-octopus, hoping to use it as a secret weapon. But then the beast escapes and goes on a killing spree off the Mexican resort city of Puerto Vallarta.

Weird as it sounds, a similar creature is said to inhabit the Bahamian island of Andros.

Called the Lusca, the beast resembles a multi-armed octopus with shark-like features. Adding to the mystery, the U.S. Navy maintains a secret base on Andros Island called AUTEC where, among other things, experiments in genetic engineering are rumored to be carried out.

5. The Giant Spider Invasion

This 1975 movie tells the tale of a monstrous spider that terrorizes a small Wisconsin town. The film's enormous arachnid is covered with black fur, has red glowing eyes, and snacks on humans.

Sound familiar? The "J'Ba Fofi," also known as the Congolese Giant Spider, can grow to enormous size and spin webs more than fifteen feet across.

And like its movie-monster cousin, it's covered with black fur, has glowing eyes, and can devour large animals.

6. The Hound of the Baskervilles

This Sherlock Holmes mystery has been adapted to movie and TV screens many times. Based on an Arthur Conan Doyle story, the hound of the title is a large, ghostly dog that haunts an aristocratic family.

While the famous mystery writer never disclosed his inspiration for the beast, some researchers believe it was based on the aforementioned Yell Hound, a giant dog said to wander the British countryside at night making blood-curdling wailing noises.

7. The Bermuda Depths

This haunting TV movie, first broadcast in 1978, tells the story of a young man obsessed by dreams of a creature he saw as a child —a gigantic turtle that roams the Bermuda Triangle.

Oddly enough, people have been seeing a similar creature for years, not in Bermuda, but in a lake near Fort Wayne, Indiana. The so-called "Busco" is said to have a head bigger than a human's and a shell so enormous it might weigh more than a ton.

8. The Blob

Released in 1958, this classic science fiction film marked the debut of legendary actor Steve McQueen.

A giant amoeba from outer space lands in a small Pennsylvania town and begins gorging itself on humans. As distasteful as that sounds, real blobs of flesh called "Globsters" have been washing up on the world's beaches for years.

While some claim these mysterious blobs are the remains of giant octopuses or even sea serpents, no one knows for sure what they are.

9. The Beast from 20, 000 Fathoms

This 1953 film is about a huge dragon-like monster that rampages through New York City.

Thawed out by a nuclear blast, the beast destroys Manhattan and Coney Island before a lone brave soul finally shoots a radioactive bullet into its neck, the most vulnerable spot on its body, and kills it.

Incredibly a similar monster, called the Peluda, was said to have roamed France in medieval times. Terrorizing the countryside and devouring humans and livestock alike, the Peluda seemed unstoppable until a lone brave soul cut off its tail, its most vulnerable spot, finally killing it.

10. Dune

This 1984 movie, based on the 1965 novel of the same name, features gigantic sandworms that can live forever. These monsters are so powerful they are worshiped as gods.

As mentioned a few pages back, the Olgoi-Khorkhoi, also known as the Mongolian Death Worm, is a real creature that can grow to massive size and be highly dangerous to humans.

11. Them!

Fifty million years ago, gigantic ants roamed what is now the state of Wyoming.

Scientists believe the monstrous insects may have crossed from Europe to North America during a warm period in Earth's history. But could these six-legged beasts have been the inspiration for *Them!* — one of the best science fiction films of all time?

In the movie, ants mutated by atomic testing grow to enormous size and build a nest under Los Angeles, sparking a war with the U.S. Army. Released in 1954, *Them* is considered Hollywood's first "big bug" film.

12. Food of the Gods

In this 1976 film, food that magically appears on a remote Canadian island is consumed by rats, turning them into murderous giants. Only when the movie's hero floods the island with water and drowns the bloated vermin are its inhabitants saved.

While monstrous rats might seem too nightmarish, remember that back in 2013 a rat found living under a sporting goods store in the Bronx was so big, it was dubbed Ratosaurus.

13. Night of the Lepus

Released in 1972, this film pits a small Arizona town against a swarm of giant killer rabbits.

Mutated by the misuse of deadly chemicals, the murderous bunnies are finally stopped when they are herded into a giant pit and machine-gunned to death.

But as it turns out, five million years ago, enormous rabbits were a reality. Called Nuralagus Rex, meaning

King of the Rabbits, they were more than six times the size of modern rabbits.

14. It Came from Beneath the Sea

This 1955 film begins with a submarine colliding with a giant octopus and ends with the massive creature attacking the Golden Gate Bridge before getting obliterated by a nuclear torpedo.

While not large enough to take on the Golden Gate Bridge, the Enteroctopus dofleini is a giant version of the familiar eight-armed sea creature. Found mostly in the northern Pacific, these beasts can grow up to twenty-five feet long and weigh more than 150-pounds.

A Monster by Any Other Name

Adolf Hitler

He claimed to be psychic and boasted that was the reason he was able to survive more than 40 assassination attempts during his reign over Nazi Germany.

The truth is, Hitler had his own personal security regimen. He knew most assassination attempts were timed to the target's schedule, so he lived his life irregularly. He routinely avoided routine. He changed established schedules at the last moment. He would not show up where he was supposed to be, then suddenly appear somewhere else.

He lived by this quote: "Walk, drive, and travel at irregular times and do so unexpectedly."

To civilization's bad luck, his formula worked perfectly.

Here are fifteen examples of how close we came to destroying a monster.

1. When Nature Called

In 1929, a German soldier planted a bomb under Hitler's speaker's platform minutes before the Fuehrer was to give a speech.

Because Hitler's speeches usually lasted for hours, the soldier visited the bathroom, certain he'd get back in time to set off the bomb. Unfortunately, the soldier became locked in the toilet and failed to get out in time to blow the Fuehrer sky high.

2. The Road Not Taken

One night in 1934, Hitler had a number of his political rivals rounded up and shot, including one of his closest colleagues, a man named Ernst Rohm.

When a group of armed Rohm supporters got the news, they confronted Hitler and his entourage on the road to Munich. Somehow Hitler persuaded the men not to shoot him and escaped; but the men had second thoughts and decided to ambush the Fuehrer farther down the road.

But Hitler ordered his driver to take another route and escaped the Grim Reaper again.

3. The Nut Behind the Wheel

In 1935, a man named Heinrich Grunow thought he'd come up with a foolproof plan to kill Hitler.

Armed with a pistol, Grunow hid himself at a spot in the road near Hitler's country retreat where he knew the Fuehrer's car had to slow down to take a turn.

As Hitler's car approached and slowed, Grunow started firing, pumping three bullets into the person in the backseat. But incredibly, he shot the wrong man.

For some reason Hitler himself was driving the car and his bodyguard/driver was riding in the back seat. As soon as the shots were fired, Hitler hit the brakes and fled on foot, leaving his dying bodyguard behind.

4. The Traveling Priest

In 1938, a Swiss seminarian named Maurice Bavaud decided to kill Hitler. Thus began a deadly game of tag between the Fuehrer and the young priest.

Once Bavaud got to Berlin, he learned Hitler was at his mountain retreat in Bavaria. Taking a train to Bavaria, Bavaud learned Hitler had left before he arrived and had returned to Berlin.

After missing a chance to shoot Hitler during a parade in Berlin, Bavaud heard that the Fuehrer had returned to Bavaria. Once again, the would-be assassin took a train to Bavaria only to learn Hitler was actually in Munich.

Bavaud then traveled to Munich, only to learn that Hitler's private train had just left for Bavaria. At that point, Bavaud finally gave up, but was later caught by the Gestapo carrying plans to assassinate the Fuehrer.

He was tried, found guilty, and beheaded.

5. The Hole in the Pillar

Every November, Hitler would attend a rally in a Munich beer hall commemorating his first attempt to seize power in 1923. Typically, he'd give a long, impassioned speech and then stay for hours to reminisce with his long-standing comrades about the old days.

Despite high security around the hall weeks ahead of time, in 1939, a carpenter named George Elser was able to slip through the phalanx of guards and gain access to the location.

In fact, he stole into the hall on 35 separate occasions using a hole he'd cut in a pillar to conceal himself and work on the bomb he'd hidden there to go off during Hitler's speech.

On the night of the rally, Hitler arrived as scheduled, but gave only a brief speech, one much shorter than in previous years. Then the Fuehrer left immediately, refusing to stay around to ruminate with his old friends. Thirteen minutes later, Elser's bomb went off, killing eight and injuring dozens.

Hitler had defied the odds again.

6. The Victory Parade

In July 1940, several German military officers assigned to occupied France decided to kill Hitler. Once the French had officially surrendered, plans were made for a victory parade in Paris during which the Fuehrer would review his conquering army.

The rebellious officers planned to shoot Hitler as he was standing on the reviewing stand, but once again, Hitler's instincts kicked in.

He abruptly canceled the parade, and instead toured Paris early that morning, seeing the sights and returning to Germany before the plotters even knew their plan had been short-circuited.

7. Not A Second Time

In May 1941, the same German officers again tried to kill Hitler.

Another parade was scheduled for Paris during which the Fuehrer would review German SS divisions serving in occupied France. The plan was for one of the officers to shoot Hitler point-blank in the head. If that failed, another officer was assigned to throw a bomb at the Fuehrer.

However, Hitler's luck came through again when, at the last minute, he declined to make the trip to Paris.

8. Unexpectedly Frozen Out

In March 1943, two other German officers plotted to kill Hitler by blowing up his private airplane while in flight.

Disguising a time bomb to look like two bottles of cognac, they planned to give the package to someone flying with Hitler, asking them to deliver it to another officer in Berlin. After one aborted attempt, the officers managed to give the package to a passenger who would be riding with the Fuehrer back to the German capital.

The plane took off and the would-be assassins awaited word of the explosion. But the unwitting passenger had placed the package in an unheated storage compartment instead of up front with Hitler, causing the bomb's timing mechanism to freeze and malfunction.

The Fuehrer had escaped death again.

9. The Snub

Later in March 1943, a German officer named Rudolf von Gersdorff was chosen to give Hitler a private tour of captured Russian weapons stored in the Berlin Armory.

But von Gersdorff detested the Fuehrer and decided to kill him via a suicide mission. Knowing the tour would last at least twenty minutes, von Gersdorff planned to carry two bombs in his pockets. Once he got close to Hitler, he would put the Fuehrer in a bear hug and then set off the bombs. It seemed like a foolproof plan.

Hitler arrived at the armory as scheduled. But to everyone's amazement, when the tour began, the Fuehrer completely ignored von Gersdorff, quickly walked past the weapons, and then went back out the door.

10. *Du wirst erblinden!*

In early 1944, a group of OSS operatives (precursors to the CIA) came up with a bizarre plan to drive Hitler to suicide.

Their idea was to fly over Hitler's Bavarian mountain headquarters and bomb it, not with explosives but with pornographic materials, hoping the notoriously puritanical Hitler would see the porn, go mad, and do himself in.

The OSS men gathered a huge amount of pornographic material to be dropped, but when they approached the U.S. Army Air Force about lending them a plane for the mission, the Brass was not impressed. The strange assassination attempt never went any further.

11. Invitation Revoked

Eberhard von Breitenbuch was a German officer who wanted Hitler dead.

In March 1944, a similar-minded officer arranged for von Breitenbuch to become an aide to a high German general, this in hopes he could get close to Hitler.

That opportunity arrived when von Breitenbuch's general was called to a meeting with the Fuehrer and von Breitenbuch was invited to go with him. Von Breitenbuch planned to shoot Hitler in the head with a pistol concealed in his pants.

Though Hitler sent a plane for the pair and von Breitenbuch was allowed into Hitler's headquarters, SS guards had been ordered by Hitler earlier that day not to permit aides into his conference room. No explanation was ever given for this unusual order.

But once again, Hitler was saved from an assassin.

12. Bombing with Bombs

In June 1944, while Nazi officers and German assassins were trying to kill Hitler with hidden pistols and pocket explosives, the U.S. Army Air Force wanted to send a couple of hundred B-17s to demolish the Fuehrer's Bavarian headquarters with tons of high explosives.

But the plan stalled after a disagreement with the British over just how the bombing raid should be executed. Instead, the Americans bombed a hotel in Milan, Italy, after getting information that Hitler was staying there. But Hitler was in East Prussia at the time.

13. Bomb in the Briefcase

Invited to a briefing on July 20, 1944 at Hitler's Wolf Lair headquarters, a German officer named Claus von Stauffenberg arrived carrying a briefcase containing two small bombs.

Though Stauffenberg was able to arm only one of the bombs, he did manage to place the briefcase under a conference table, close to Hitler, before excusing himself and leaving the room.

But the briefcase was moved by another officer, placing it farther away from the Fuehrer. When the bomb went off, Hitler was shielded by the heavy conference table and was only slightly wounded.

Stauffenberg was quickly arrested and executed. Eight other conspirators were strangled with piano wire; their deaths were filmed and allegedly drooled over by Hitler.

Because Hitler used the July 20 plot as an excuse to eliminate anyone he suspected of opposing him, more than 20,000 Germans were killed or sent to concentration camps.

14. Not at Home

In April 1945, the British decided to bomb Hitler's mountaintop headquarters on its own.

In one of the RAF's last missions of the war, 350 bombers dropped more than five million pounds of bombs on the complex of buildings that made up Hitler's country home.

There were many direct hits, and the retreat was virtually leveled.

But Hitler was in Berlin at the time.

15. <u>A Little Tooty</u>

Hitler took so many drugs on a daily, sometimes hourly, basis — cocaine and amphetamines, among them — it's a wonder he didn't OD. Or maybe gas himself to death. A combination of a nervous stomach and militant vegetarianism led to a 15-year condition Hitler's personal physician once described as "colossal flatulence on a scale I have seldom encountered before."

Weird Warships

What's in a Name?

Commissioned in 1890, USS *Vesuvius* was the only American warship ever to be outfitted with dynamite guns.

Its three pneumatic cannons could fire 500-pound high-explosive shells at targets up to a mile away. They were used during the Spanish-American War in 1898 to bombard enemy positions in Cuba.

What made them even more sinister, the TNT shells were propelled by compressed air, meaning there was little sound when they were fired, surprising enemies used to hearing massive booms indicating incoming fire. But dynamite cannons were not known for accuracy, and they required a lot of maintenance.

The *Vesuvius's* TNT guns were eventually removed and replaced with torpedo tubes. The ship later almost sank itself when one it its torpedoes malfunctioned after launch, turned three hundred sixty degrees, and slammed into its hull.

Project Azorian

While the *Glomar Explorer* was officially known as a maritime geology research ship, in reality, it was a top-secret submarine recovery vessel.

The ship was designed to raise the Soviet submarine K-129, which sank in the Pacific in 1968. The Soviets had been unsuccessful in locating its wreckage and assumed the submarine came to rest at an inaccessible depth.

However, the U.S. Navy managed to find the doomed sub in the early 1970s and in 1974, the CIA launched Project Azorian. Its goal was to secretly recover the K-129 from the sea floor along with its codebooks and nuclear missiles.

The *Glomar Explorer* had been built with a gigantic claw that could be lowered from a hole in the bottom of the ship. The CIA planned to use the claw to grab the sub and pull it to the surface.

The plan almost worked. The claw managed to clamp onto the K-129, but the sub snapped in two as it was being lifted. While half the sub was pulled into the *Glomar Explorer*, the section containing all the secrets fell back to the ocean floor and was deemed unsalvageable.

Or so the CIA claims.

This project was so secret that when then President Richard Nixon saw the ship during a tour of Naval Base San Diego and asked for a tour, the CIA turned him down.

The Lonely Aircraft Carrier

In 1912, the world's largest side-wheel steamer was launched. It was named the *Seeandbee.*

Little did its builders know that 40 years later, their creation would become a most unusual warship.

Acquired by the Navy in 1942 and renamed the USS *Wolverine*, the paddle boat was converted into an aircraft carrier. But it never saw action. In fact, it never even saw the ocean.

Operating in Lake Michigan, the *Wolverine* provided a platform for rookie Navy pilots to practice takeoffs and landings before heading to the Pacific to fight the Japanese.

However, carrier ops require two things: wind and vessel speed. A general lack of wind on Lake Michigan combined with the inability of the *Wolverine's* paddle wheel to generate sufficient speed resulted in many accidents.

At least 60 Navy airplanes are still believed to be at the bottom of Lake Michigan as a result.

The *Wolverine* and another training carrier, the USS *Sable*, were decommissioned at war's end and eventually scrapped.

Comrade, in Circles We Are Going

After getting beat in the Crimean War in 1856, Russia rebuilt its Black Sea Fleet in hopes of defeating the navies of France and Britain should they ever come calling again.

To this end, in 1874, Russia launched one of history's strangest-looking warships. In a word, the *Novgorod* was *circular.* Built that way presumably for stability, the ship weighed 2,490 tons and had a diameter of 100 feet. It had an armored turret containing two twelve-inch guns sitting on a turntable that could turn 35-degrees in either direction. The ship had six engines, each of which spun one propeller.

Russia built a second circular ship in 1877, the bigger *Vice-Admiral Popov*. It weighed in at 3,550 tons and had a diameter of 120 feet.

These two ships had a radical design, but not a successful one. They often floundered even in calm water. But more distressing, they tended to spin in circles when the engines were in idle, not a pleasant feeling at sea.

For some reason though, the czar loved the concept and ordered the building of a circular royal yacht.

Military historian Stanley Sandler once said this must have been because the czar "presumably suffered more from seasickness than dizziness."

You Can't Make This Up

At one time or another, the British Royal Navy had warships named HMS Dainty, HMS Pansy, HMS Cockchafer, and HMS Spanker.

Brave New World: Part 1

What are you … high?

New York City

While New York's water supply is considered extremely clean, a study done several years ago found many of the rivers and streams that feed the Big Apple's reservoirs contain high levels of flushed drugs, including many sedatives and antidepressants.

This has prompted some to suggest changing the city's nickname to The Big Happy.

Southern California

Although Los Angeles County is among the country's leaders in recycling sewage back into drinking water, anti-epileptic and anti-anxiety drugs were recently found in surprisingly high numbers in LA's water supply.

Minnesota

Known as the Land of 10,000 Lakes, Minnesota seems postcard-perfect when it comes to pristine water.

Yet officials there were astonished a few years back to find inexplicably high levels of cocaine in more than a third of the state's water supply.

Philadelphia

More than five-dozen different pharmaceuticals or their byproducts were discovered in Philly's water supply back in 2012. These included medications prescribed for heart problems, pain, infections, asthma, epilepsy, and mental illness.

Crack

When the crack cocaine epidemic exploded in the 1980s, it hit the poor neighborhoods of south central Los Angeles especially hard — and there might be a dark reason why.

At least one prominent newspaper at the time claimed that leaders of Nicaragua's Contra movement were supplying vast amounts of cocaine to drug dealers in LA with the approval and cooperation of the CIA. The profits from this illegal drug trade, the newspaper claimed, went to buy weapons for the anti-communist Contras.

Weed

With many states now allowing recreational pot sales and many others permitting its purchase for medical reasons, marijuana seems headed for eventual nationwide legalization.

But why? Is it because these state governments have realized the futility of jailing pot smokers for something considered less dangerous than drinking or cigarette smoking?

Or is it because, by some estimates, legalized pot sales would result in hundreds of billions of dollars in tax revenues?

Uncle Sam Wants You Tripping

While most people associate LSD with the hippie culture of the 1960s, the CIA was secretly dosing unwitting Americans with the hallucinogenic drug back in the '50s.

According to documents revealed many years later, one way the CIA did this was by paying prostitutes to slip LSD into their customers' drinks and then luring them back to specially prepared apartments where agents observed their reactions through one-way mirrors.

The reason for this was that the CIA believed the Russians and Communist Chinese would use LSD to brainwash captured American soldiers and the Agency wanted to fully understand the drug's effects for their own brainwashing programs.

This practice was finally halted in 1964.

Uncle Sam Wants You Gay

Fringe talk-show host Alex Jones once claimed that demonic forces within the U.S. government are lining the packaging of juice drinks, water bottles, and potato chip bags with chemicals that will turn American children gay.

The reason for such a plot, Jones contends, is that with more gay people, there will be fewer children, and a smaller population will make it easier for the One World conspiracists inside our government to seize control of the United States.

Fluoride

Many U.S. municipalities have added fluoride to their drinking water since the 1950s to reduce tooth decay in adults and children.

But many people oppose fluoridation, some saying it amounts to nothing less than an involuntary dosing of the American population. Others claim that it's a long-running communist plot to brainwash us.

Caffeine

Most Americans get their caffeine fix from coffee, soda, or tea — but many ingest massive amounts of this stimulant drug via energy drinks.

The maximum recommended daily intake of caffeine equals about four cups of coffee, yet some energy drinks contain that much caffeine in just one eight-ounce can.

And while overuse of caffeine can cause heart issues, anxiety, sleep disorders, muscle tremors, and even certain kinds of mania, sales of energy drinks in the U.S. have reached $1 billion a year.

Nicotine

A stimulant drug found in many tobacco products, nicotine is not only highly addictive, it's one of the hardest addictions to break — considered on the same scale as heroin and cocaine. Yet studies show that cigarette manufacturers have quietly raised the amount of nicotine in their products over the years, with nicotine content in cigarettes nearly 20 percent higher now than just a decade ago.

Roofies

Though banned in the U.S., Rohyprol, a drug used as an anesthetic in other parts of the world, has made its way into this country and is sold illegally in pill form.

Called the "date rape" drug, it can be slipped into a person's drink surreptitiously, causing semi-consciousness and memory blackouts, which can then lead to unwanted sexual encounters.

Thankfully, though, some studies show that wide-spread use of "roofies" in the U.S. is more urban myth than reality.

UFOs Behaving Badly

Sometimes they're as squishy as an ET doll.
Sometimes, they're not.

I found these stories while researching *UFOs in Wartime* and *Beyond Area 51*.

Colares Island, Brazil

There is chilling evidence that in 1977, this island off the northeast coast of Brazil was attacked by flying saucers. Coming out of the night, the mystery craft fired laser-like beams at the island's population, killing two and injuring nearly a hundred.

The onslaught was so severe the Brazilian military conducted an amazingly thorough investigation of the incident. But exactly what happened that night has never been determined.

Dark Skies Above

As we know, the top-secret Russian military base at Kapustin Yar is a combination of Cape Canaveral and Area 51.

Like its American counterpart, this installation, which is close to Volgograd in southern Russia, boasts numerous "unidentified areas," buildings whose purpose can only be guessed at.

Also like Area 51, Kapustin Yar has a history of UFO incidents.

Russian UFO enthusiasts claim that the first extraterrestrial dogfight happened at Kapustin Yar in 1948. While guiding a Soviet fighter plane in for landing, the base's radar station reportedly picked up a UFO flying close by. Quickly alerting the plane by radio, its pilot was said to have spotted the strange object as well. He described it as being silver in color and shaped like a cigar.

As the story goes, word of what was happening was flashed directly to Soviet leader Josef Stalin. Probably believing the object was a spy plane sent from the West, Stalin ordered the fighter plane to shoot it down.

But it was not as simple as that.

When the Russian pilot attacked as ordered, a prolonged aerial battle ensued. The UFO and the Russian airplane began blazing away at each other, firing their respective weapons as they twisted and turned through the sky. It took a while, but finally both sides scored what turned out to be mortal blows.

Both craft eventually crashed, and while the fate of the Soviet pilot was never revealed, multiple sources say the UFO's debris and possibly the bodies of its occupants were recovered and hidden away at Kapustin Yar.

Close Encounter in Korea

Early in the spring of 1951, U.S. Army Private Francis Wall found himself on the slope of a mountain near Chorwon, North Korea.

Wall's unit was fighting the communists for control of a village below. It was while they were shelling the village that something very strange happened.

"We suddenly noticed on our right-hand side, what appeared to be a jack-o-lantern come wafting across the mountain," Wall told UFO researcher Dr. Richard Haines years later. "This thing continued on down to the village where our artillery bursts were exploding. It had an orange glow in the beginning. We further noticed it could get into the center of an airburst of artillery and yet remain unharmed."

Wall and his fellow soldiers watched the astonishing object for about thirty minutes. Then its disposition suddenly changed.

"This object approached us," Wall said. "It turned a brilliant blue-green and started pulsating."

Wall and his comrades became so alarmed they asked their commanding officer for permission to fire at the object. The request was quickly granted.

"I fired at it with an M-1 rifle with armor-piercing bullets," Wall said. "And I hit it. It must have been metallic, because you could hear the projectiles slamming into it. But why would a bullet damage this craft if the artillery rounds didn't? I don't know. But after I hit it, the object went wild. The light was going on and off. It was moving erratically from side to side, as though it might crash. Then, a sound — we had heard no sound previous to this — the sound of diesel locomotives revving up. That's the way this thing sounded."

Things quickly went from bad to worse for the shocked GIs.

"We were attacked," Wall said. "We were swept by some form of ray. It was like a searchlight. You would feel a burning, tingling sensation all over your body (when it hit you), as though something were penetrating you."

"So the company commander hauled us into our bunkers. We didn't know what was going to happen. We were scared. These are underground dugouts where you have peepholes to look out to fire at the enemy. So, I'm in my bunker with another man. We're peeping out at this thing. It hovered over us for a while, lit up the whole area with its light, and then I saw it shoot off at a 45-degree angle, that quick, just there and gone."

But this was not the end of it for Private Walls and his colleagues. Three days later, Wall's unit had to be evacuated from the battlefield. Roads were cut so the soldiers could be taken out by ambulance. Many were too weak to walk.

When Army physicians examined them, they were all found to have extremely elevated white blood cell counts, a serious condition that doctors had no explanation for.

The Haunted Highway

On January 20, 1988, Fay Knowles and her three sons set out from the city of Perth in Western Australia, heading for Melbourne in the east. Their mode of transportation was a 1984 Ford sedan. Their route took them across the notorious Nullarbor Plain.

Connecting South and Western Australia, the Nullarbor Plain runs for more than 1000 miles east to west. It's mostly flat, arid desert, and as its Latin name suggests, it's practically treeless. The Eyre Highway, which features the longest straight stretch of road in the world (90 miles without a bend or curve), is its main highway.

Crossing the Nullarbor Plain can be hazardous. Run out of gas or have a mechanical problem and your car will likely join the many abandoned vehicles that can be found along the way. At the very least you'll have a long walk ahead of you.

But the Nullarbor Plain is known for something even more unpleasant than breakdowns in the middle of nowhere. Some of the most frightening UFO incidents ever reported have happened here, as the Knowles family was about to find out.

Driving through the Nullarbor at night, when it was cooler, the Knowleses had proceeded on their trip incident-free. But just before four in the morning, the family saw a bright light on the road ahead of them. Sean Knowles, twenty-one, was driving.

Everyone in the car assumed the light was just a truck coming in the opposite direction. But then the light began moving erratically. It would disappear only to reappear an instant later, much closer to the Knowles's car. After it happened a few times, Sean floored the accelerator. The light disappeared, only to wind up behind them.

Sean hit the gas once more, this time to get away. But an instant later, the bright light was in front of them again. The family finally realized this thing was a solid flying object, and it was now blinding them with its intense bright light. Still, Sean was able to turn the car one hundred-eighty degrees, intent on speeding away in the opposite direction.

But the object stayed with them. Sean performed another U-turn, nearly colliding with a car coming in the opposite direction, but again the object persisted in chasing them.

Then the family heard a loud thud on the roof of their car. Something had landed there! Though panic-stricken, Mrs. Knowles rolled down her window and reached up to the roof, only to feel something warm and spongy. When she pulled her hand back inside, it was covered with hot black soot. An instant later, the car was filled with a black mist that stunk of rotting flesh, accompanied by a painful high-pitched sound. Most bizarre of all, the family's voices became lower in pitch and their speech started to slow down.

With all four family members beyond terrified, the object began *lifting* their car off the roadway. It carried the Ford a short distance before slamming it back down to the pavement with such force that one of its tires blew out.

Somehow, Sean managed to pull to the side of the road, where the family scrambled out and hid in some bushes. They watched as the object hovered around their disabled car for a few moments before taking off at tremendous speed. Eventually the family summoned up the courage to put on their spare tire and flee to the nearby town of Mundrabilla.

Luckily for them, they met three witnesses who'd also seen the strange object out on Eyre Highway. Returning to the scene of the incident, one witness found skid marks and located the Ford's blown-out tire. When police questioned the family members, they found them severely traumatized. They were convinced something truly bizarre had happened to them.

But theirs was not an isolated case. So many cars have been chased by flying objects along the Nullarbor Plain that one local government erected a sign warning motorists to "Beware of the UFOs."

F-16 vs. UFO

This incident involves an F-16 fighter jet dogfighting and then shooting down a UFO over Saudi Arabia at the height of the first Gulf War.

The principal purveyor of the episode is a shadowy Russian colonel worthy of a James Bond novel. The Russian officer just happened to be in Riyadh, the capital of Saudi Arabia, when the shoot-down took place. He claimed to be one of the first people to know the location of the UFO's crash, which was deep in the Saudi desert, some 250 miles northeast of Riyadh.

Saudi radar technicians told the Russian officer the details of the air battle. Four U.S. Air Force F-16s were on a mission to Baghdad when an unidentified blip appeared on their radar screens. As the Saudi technicians watched, one of the F-16s left the formation and started chasing the UFO. The UFO changed direction in an attempt to escape, but the F-16 continued in pursuit. The UFO then apparently fired a weapon at the F-16 but missed. The F-16 returned fire with two missiles, and both hit the craft. The UFO blew up and its wreckage went down in flames.

The Saudis said no one was seen ejecting from the stricken craft. But even though helicopters scoured the area over the crash site, no bodies or survivors were found.

The Russian colonel said the U.S. immediately tried to cover up the incident, saying it never happened. But upon reaching the crash site and seeing the wreckage for himself, the officer knew it was not from any earthly aircraft. He estimated that about one-third of the object had been destroyed by the American missiles, leaving the rest scattered on the desert floor.

The colonel described the downed craft as having been circular and built of some unrecognizable material. It was about fifteen feet long and, judging by its seats, built for someone, or *something*, of small stature. The Russian says he saw instruments, machinery, and other things that defied description. These included markings on the instrument panels that were written in some indecipherable language. The Saudis who accompanied him to the crash site were so frightened by the strange debris, and what it might mean, that they asked American investigators to come to the crash site immediately.

When the U.S. military finally arrived, the Russian colonel said he and his colleagues were immediately ordered out of the area. They were eventually flown back to Riyadh.

The colonel was reported to have said, "There were things the Americans didn't want us to see."

And though his comrades were able to surreptitiously take photographs of the UFO's wreckage, the next day, the colonel was ordered by authorities from his own country to turn over all photos of the crash site to them.

The colonel said he learned later that the U.S. Army eventually gathered up the crash debris, put it into crates, and flew it all back to the United States.

My Top Ten Favorite Stories from 'UFOs in Wartime'

1. Medieval Air Battle

On April 4, 1561, the citizens of Nuremberg, Germany, awoke to a titanic air battle going on over their city.

Hundreds of witnesses saw a pair of large, dark cylinders spewing a variety of shapes variously described as black-and-blue spheres, red crosses, and aerial disks. Once launched, the objects fought each other for more than an hour.

This incredible event was reported by The Nuremberg Gazette, and an artist named Hans Glaser did a woodcut depicting the frenzied battle.

What would have spurred this newspaper story and woodcut if not a real event?

2. The Ray Smith Incident

On May 27, 1943, a Royal Air Force Halifax bomber was heading to Essen, Germany, as part of a massive nighttime bombing raid. Its pilot was Ray Smith of the Royal Canadian Air Force.

Flying at 19,000 feet, Smith had no trouble finding the target. Essen had been bombed by the RAF earlier that evening, and the light from the resulting flames could be seen for hundreds of miles.

Smith's Halifax arrived over the target to find the sky filed with antiaircraft fire. As he was preparing for his bombing run, the pilot noticed something strange flying off his left wing. It was a silver-gold cylindrical object and it was moving through the flak-filled sky at the same speed and altitude as the bomber.

Smith's crew had spotted it, too. It was much bigger than the Halifax and had portholes evenly spaced along its length.

The astonished airmen watched the object for almost a minute before it abruptly climbed away and disappeared into the night.

3. Giants Over Korea

One early morning in September 1950, just two months into the Korean War, three U.S. Navy fighter-bombers were headed for the communist north. Each plane carried a pilot, a radar operator/gunner, and several tons of bombs.

Their mission was to attack a North Korean truck convoy that had been seen moving through a valley 100 miles south of the Chinese border.

Spotting the convoy, the Navy crews began preparing for their bombing runs when they were astonished to see a pair of gigantic saucer-shaped objects approaching from the northwest. The silver-colored disks were at least seven hundred feet in diameter —more than two football fields put together — and were traveling close to Mach 2, or 1,200 mph, twice as fast as any aircraft of the day.

The monstrous saucers stopped in midair, changed direction, and came right at the three Navy planes. Instinctively, the Navy gunners tried to fire on them, but found their weapons jammed. In seconds, the mammoth disks were effortlessly circling the fighter-bombers, as if inspecting them.

Then just as abruptly, the saucers turned back to the northwest and left the area at high speed.

4. The Haneda Incident

On August 5, 1952, just before midnight, air traffic control operators inside the tower of Haneda Air Force Base, a former American installation that is now Tokyo International Airport, spotted an incredibly bright light northeast of nearby Tokyo Bay.

It was not a star — these men had spent many hours looking up at the night sky; they knew a star when they saw one. As if to confirm this, they realized the light was actually moving; in fact, it was coming right at them.

The men began examining the mysterious light through powerful binoculars. The object was getting closer to the airbase and becoming more distinct, with a top and a bottom and lights illuminated in between.

Suddenly the UFO moved east, out of view of the control tower. But just as quickly, it appeared again. It stayed in sight for a few moments and then vanished again. But then it returned.

What was going on? What were all these strange movements?

The tower operators called a nearby radar station, and asked if they were picking up anything on their screens. As it turned out, they were. What the tower operators were seeing visually, the radar men were seeing electronically.

Meanwhile, the UFO continued acting strangely, moving back and forth above Tokyo Bay, sometimes hovering motionless and sometimes speeding up to more than 300 mph.

An F-94 interceptor was scrambled from a nearby base and arrived over Haneda. Seconds later, the F-94's backseat radar man got a lock on the object about three miles in front of the jet. The fighter plane began pursuing the object.

The tower personnel watched as the F-94 and the UFO made a wide turn together. At that point, the object accelerated away from the F-94 and the tower operators lost sight of it.

The fighter stayed around another few minutes but found nothing else. It returned to its base. As soon as it departed, the UFO reappeared.

The tower personnel kept it in sight for another two minutes, when suddenly the UFO broke into three separate pieces. The three pieces left the area at high speed, and that ended the episode.

In all, the UFO had been in sight or tracked on radar for more than thirty minutes.

The Haneda sighting fascinated Captain Edward Ruppelt, the officer in charge of Project Blue Book, the U.S. Air Force unit created in March 1952 ostensibly to look into UFOs.

The back-and-forth movements of the object reminded Ruppelt of flight patterns used by aircraft when searching for someone at sea. Rescue aircraft fly in preassigned grids, covering as much area as they can in the least amount of time. Did UFOs ever move like that? Or did they simply fly through the air in random fashion?

It was an important question. Random motion would be similar to a swarm of bees, with no pattern or purpose to their flight paths. But in a case like a flock of geese, flying in a chevron, there is a defined pattern to their movements — and a defined pattern would indicate intelligent control.

Ruppelt came to the conclusion that doing an extensive motion study of UFO maneuvers would be a great way to advance research into the phenomena. But as usual, the Air Force had other ideas. Those people in the Pentagon who could have actually funded such a study turned him down cold.

Later on, the Colorado Project, a skeptical UFO study effort with ties to the USAF, determined that the Haneda sighting was nothing more than false radar echoes caused by a temperature inversion layer.

5. Chilling Tale from the Cold War

In 1951, the U.S. Air Force's 525th Fighter Bomber Squadron was based at Neubiberg, West Germany. Located near Munich, the squadron was a short flight from the border of then communist-controlled Czechoslovakia.

Tensions were high around the world in 1951. Germany was split in two, the communist East staring down the democratic West. Russia now had atomic weapons and its client state, North Korea, had invaded U.S. ally South Korea the year before. All-out war with the Communist Bloc seemed inevitable.

The pilots of the 525th flew the F-86 Sabre jet; its communist adversaries just over the border were equipped with MiG-15s. Always on combat alert, the 525th was frequently scrambled whenever MiGs were detected too close to the border of West Germany.

So it was one particular day when a virtual armada of unidentified aircraft was spotted heading toward West Germany. The 525th was quickly airborne, its pilots climbing to meet what they were sure was an onslaught of Russian MiGs.

But when the Sabres reached their maximum altitude of 45,000 feet, their pilots discovered the horde of bogeys were not Russian fighters. This air fleet was made up of metallic objects, shaped like saucers. And there were lots of them.

The objects were flying way too high for the Sabres to challenge them, so the 525th's pilots could do little more than watch as the swarm of UFOs passed overhead.

Flying one of those Sabres that day was a young second lieutenant named Gordon Cooper. As he would later tell it, streams of UFOs went over the 525th's base regularly for the next three days. Sometimes they were in groups of four, other times in groups of as many as sixteen. They were almost always traveling from east to west.

Besides flying so high, the UFOs displayed high degrees of maneuverability. They would sometimes move at very high speed; other times, they would hover motionless as the fighters of the 525th simply flew beneath them, helpless.

Finally, the 525th gave up trying to intercept them. Instead, the pilots would stay on the ground and use binoculars to watch the UFOs pass high overhead. After a while it became the opinion of Cooper and just about anyone who'd seen them that these objects had not been made in Russia, China, or anywhere else on Earth.

But even though word of the daily parade of UFOs was passed up to the highest levels of the Pentagon, no official investigation was ever undertaken to determine what they were.

Gordon Cooper gradually rose up the ranks of the Air Force, becoming an outstanding fighter pilot and then a test pilot. He was such a talented aviator, eight years later he would be selected as one of America's first astronauts.

But those strange days back at the beginning of the decade would not be his last experience with UFOs.

6. The Incredible Gander Sighting

One of the most dramatic UFO sightings ever occurred on February 10, 1956, over the Atlantic Ocean.

At the time, the U.S. Navy had an airplane called the R7V-2 transport. A military version of the Lockheed Super Constellation, it had four propellers and a distinctive tri-fin tail wing. It could carry about 90 passengers or several tons of cargo.

This particular R7V-2 had left Keflavik, Iceland, after refueling and was heading for Gander Air Force Base in Newfoundland with the eventual destination of the Navy air station at Patuxent River, Maryland.

The plane was flying at 19,000 feet and the night was clear. The pilot was a U.S. Navy commander, a 10-year veteran who'd made the Atlantic crossing more than 200 times. There were 30 U.S. military personnel on board the flight, including several aircrews. Most of these passengers were heading home after duty overseas.

About 90 miles from Gander, the pilot looked out on the ocean below and, instead of seeing complete darkness as usual, he saw a clutch of bright lights about 25 miles in front of him.

The pilot pointed this out to his copilot, who saw the lights too. The pilot was sure the lights were coming from a village. But if that were true, then the plane must have been over land, which meant it was wildly off course.

The plane's navigator disagreed, though; his instruments said they were directly on course. He suggested the lights might be a gathering of ships, possibly something to do with a special military operation.

The pilot then asked his radioman if he was picking up any chatter from any ships nearby. His answer was no.

The other flight crews riding in back of the plane were asked to come up to the cockpit. The pilot wanted them to see the lights, hoping one of them might have an answer to the mystery.

With these men in place, the pilot banked the large plane so everyone could get a better look. Suddenly the lights below dimmed, to be replaced by several expanding colored rings.

As the aircrews watched in astonishment, one of these rings began getting bigger. In the next instant, everyone in the crowded cockpit realized this ring was not floating on the sea. It was actually rushing up toward the transport plane.

The pilot hastily pulled out of his bank and started climbing as fast as the plane would allow — but it was no use. This colored ring was on them in seconds. Only then was it clear the ring was actually the rim of a gigantic, saucer-shaped craft, one that dwarfed the Navy plane.

In fact, the saucer was nearly five times larger than the R7V-2 — meaning it was at least 600 feet across and 30 feet thick.

The gigantic saucer very nearly collided with the transport plane. It had climbed almost five miles in less than eight seconds, meaning it was moving somewhere between 2,000 and 2,200 mph. But somehow, the craft's tremendous speed abruptly dissipated, and a collision was avoided.

Suddenly, the giant saucer was riding off the plane's wing, not 300 feet away. The two craft flew like this for a short while. Then the monstrous saucer accelerated to tremendous speed and, in an instant, was gone, disappearing into the night.

Regaining his composure, the pilot radioed the Gander air base, which said it had picked up an unidentified blip but had failed to get it on the radio.

The pilot gave Gander a short version of what had just happened and then proceeded as quickly as possible to the air base. When the transport plane landed, several Air Force intelligence officers were on hand to greet it.

They immediately began questioning the crew, but it was obvious to the Navy pilot from the start that their interrogators were not surprised that the transport plane had come in contact with the huge saucer. In the two hours of extensive questioning that followed, the Air

Force men wanted to know details, like how close the saucer had come to the transport and whether the plane's crew had encountered any electrical interference during the encounter, questions that indicated they'd been through this before.

The R7V-2 transport eventually made its way to its destination of Pax River air station. Here, the passengers were interrogated again, this time by Navy intelligence officers. Only then were the passengers free to go, no doubt told not to mention to anybody what had occurred over the Atlantic.

About a week after the incident, the transport plane's pilot got a call from a scientist working for a high-level U.S. government agency. The scientist wanted to question the pilot about the saucer incident.

The Navy had cleared the scientist to talk to the pilot, and a meeting was set up for the next day.

The scientist listened to the pilot's version of the encounter. Then, at the end of the session, the scientist took out a folder that contained photographs of UFOs.

He showed the photos to the pilot, asking if he recognized any of them. According to the pilot, the third photo showed exactly what he and his colleagues had seen that night. The pilot was astonished that the scientist, and by extension, the U.S. government, had an exact photo of the object.

The pilot demanded the scientist tell him where he'd gotten the photo. His rationale was if the U.S. government had a photo of what he saw, then someone must know what it was.

But the scientist said nothing.

According to the pilot, the man just gathered up his photos and left without another word.

7. A Circle Is Completed

On the morning of May 3, 1957, a film crew at Edwards Air Force Base was tasked with filming a new piece of equipment near one of the base's runways. The crew consisted of two enlisted men, both trained photographers and experienced at shooting pictures at the vast air base.

Located in the desert on the far eastern edge of Los Angeles County, Edwards was then, and still is, the holy land for America's military aviators. Its official name is the Air Force Flight Test Center and, as such, it's a gathering place for this country's elite test pilots.

Many of the U.S. military's experimental aircraft have been flight-tested here over the years. Because the air base is located next to an enormous dry lakebed, its runways literally extend for miles, a necessity when flying new, advanced, and unpredictable airframes.

Edwards is also a highly restricted place. All of its activities are classified. Security breaches here are considered on the same level as those at Area 51, several hundred miles to the northeast in the Nevada desert. In fact, technically speaking, Area 51 is an extension of Edwards AFB.

The two enlisted men were filming a new precision landing system. Their equipment consisted of a specialized camera designed to take one frame a second, images that would be used later to study aircraft landing characteristics.

They were also equipped with a movie camera and an ordinary still camera.

They began work at 0800 hours.

Later that morning, the two men rushed into their commanding officer's office, out of breath and extremely anxious.

They'd just seen a flying saucer — this is what they told their superior. The craft had flown right over their heads and touched down about 150 feet away, but when they tried to approach it, it took off at great speed. The object was indeed saucer-shaped, silver metallic, and had landed on three extended legs.

Given that these men were photographers, the officer's first question was obvious. "Did you get any pictures?" he asked.

They replied: "Yes, sir. We were shooting the whole time."

The officer told the men to develop the film immediately. In the meantime, he called a special number at the Pentagon used by the military for occasions such as this. The officer's first conversation was with another captain. He was then passed on to a colonel, who passed him on to a general. The general ordered him to develop the film but not to make any copies. He was then to put the film into a secure pouch and have it flown immediately to Washington, D.C., on the Edwards base commander's plane.

The officer did what the general ordered, but not before looking at the still camera's negatives. What he saw astonished him. The photos were clear, crisp, and in focus — and indeed, they showed the object landing, at rest, and taking off again. He didn't look at the motion-picture film, but he didn't have to. He knew he was looking at a flying saucer.

And that was ironic, to say the least, because this was not the officer's first brush with UFOs.

The officer was Gordon Cooper, now a captain and test pilot just a couple of years away from being selected as one of America's first astronauts.

What he'd seen up close in the photos was pretty much what he'd seen flying so high over West Germany back in 1951.

The circle was complete — or so it seemed.

Cooper said later that once the photos and film reached Washington, he was sure there would be a huge investigation and that he'd be asked about everything he knew.

But that investigation never materialized. Despite the fact that there was now photographic evidence of a flying saucer landing, in the middle of a highly classified installation, no less, the Air Force never did anything about it. There was no follow-up. In fact, no one in the military ever mentioned it to Cooper again.

To his dying day in 2004, Gordon Cooper, test pilot, astronaut, and American hero, didn't just suspect, but actually *knew* — like hundreds of other U.S. military pilots — that UFOs were real, and that throughout the 1950s the government they'd devoted their lives to had gone to great lengths to cover up their existence.

8. The Walker Sightings

Located in southeast New Mexico, Walker Air Force Base was turned into an ICBM installation in the early 1960s.

It received its first nuclear missiles starting in 1962 and, within a year, personnel assigned to the sprawling facility began seeing UFOs on a disturbingly regular basis.

One officer reported nine instances where guards saw UFOs shining bright lights down onto the base's missile silos. Though these incidents were passed on to higher authorities, the Air Force apparently did nothing about them.

In fact, right from the beginning, the Air Force seemed uninterested, reluctant, or under orders not to investigate anything having to do with UFO sightings around Walker AFB.

This baffling lack of interest was confirmed by another officer assigned to Walker, who said in the fall of 1964 that security personnel reported seeing an extremely bright light repeatedly hovering over a missile site, then racing away, returning, and hovering again. Many people witnessed this inexplicable behavior, yet the Air Force never debriefed any of them.

Still another airman at Walker contacted his superiors when he saw two star-like objects moving over his launch facility. As it turned out, the objects were already being tracked on Walker's radar, and two jet fighters from a nearby air base had been scrambled to intercept them. Witnesses even saw the jets streak toward the mysterious objects only to see the UFOs accelerate to an incredible speed and disappear. But later on, Walker's commanders not only denied the presence of UFOs that night, they even denied they'd requested jet fighters to intercept them.

But then one missile technician at Walker had an encounter with a UFO that was hard to ignore. This man was working deep inside one of the missile silos one night when a guard up top reported strange lights outside the silo's perimeter. The technician emerged from the underground facility to see a "noiseless, brilliant, and seemingly dimensionless object" had landed close to the missile site.

Flashlights in hand, the technician and the guard slowly approached the strange object, only to have it suddenly disappear. The technician later told his story to the Air Force's Office of Special Investigations, the somewhat shadowy OSI, but the man was never told whether a formal report was filed or not.

So many strange things happened at Walker during 1963 and 1964 that one worker finally contacted NICAP, the National Investigations Committee on Aerial Phenomena. In a letter written in December 1964, the worker said UFO sightings at the base had become so numerous that many guards were too frightened to go on duty. Yet the USAF insisted that everything related to the sightings should be considered top secret.

Even more troubling, at least for some hard-core believers, this worker also told NICAP that one missile silo at Walker in particular had endured many recurring UFO sightings.

That silo was Site 8, located just south of Roswell, New Mexico.

9. The Hobart Incident

This UFO incident started on the night of June 15, 1968. U.S. military observers stationed along the eastern part of Vietnam's demilitarized zone – a sort of no man's land dividing the embattled country in two -- saw strange lights moving slowly across the sky.

The observers believed the "lights" could only be North Vietnamese helicopters carrying troops and supplies across the so-called DMZ. Suspecting a new enemy offensive might be building, the U.S. military rushed large numbers of anti-aircraft weapons up to the DMZ, put U.S. Air Force fighters at Da Nang air base on high alert, and asked that all available Allied warships in the area start patrols off the DMZ's coast.

The Australian Navy destroyer *HMAS Hobart* was one of those warships.

The North Vietnamese did not fly helicopters during the Vietnam War, at least not after 1965. And even if they had, the communists would have been foolish to fly them over the DMZ and into South Vietnam's air-space, as they would quickly have been shot down by American forces. Yet the U.S. military could not come up with any other explanation for the objects spotted flying over the DMZ.

The mysterious lights reappeared the following night, once again detected moving along the eastern edge of the DMZ. Several U.S. Air Force fighter planes were dispatched, intent on engaging the intruders. U.S. antiaircraft guns also fired at the unknown aircraft. That's when the lights were seen moving off the coast and out to the sea.

At about 3:30 a.m., the *Hobart* was in position off the coast of the DMZ when its crew detected an aircraft approaching. The ship was attempting to contact the aircraft when a missile slammed into its starboard side, killing one sailor and injuring two others. Seconds later, two more missiles hit the *Hobart*, killing another sailor and injuring several more. The *Hobart's* gun crews fired on the attacker but scored no hits.

An investigation later determined that the missiles came from U.S. fighter planes whose pilots thought they were firing at the mysterious lights. The missiles missed their intended targets and hit the Australian destroyer instead. The next morning, American helicopters airlifted the injured sailors off the *Hobart*, and the heavily damaged destroyer headed to Subic Bay in the Philippines for repairs.

The late General George S. Brown was commander of the U.S. 7th Air Force at the time of the incident. He was in charge of the jet fighters involved in the *Hobart* attack.

Years later, Brown became chairman of the Joint Chiefs of Staff, the highest position in the U.S. military. In 1973, he was quoted as saying: "UFOs plagued us in Vietnam. They weren't called UFOs — they were called 'enemy helicopters.' They were only seen at night and only in certain places. They were seen up around the DMZ in the early summer of 1968, and this resulted in quite a battle. And in the course of this, an Australian destroyer took a hit. There was no enemy at all involved, but we always reacted. Always after dark."

The origin of the mysterious lights was never determined.

10. The Coyne Incident

On the night of October 18, 1973, a U.S. Army Reserve helicopter was flying from Port Columbus, Ohio, to Cleveland-Hopkins Airport.

The helicopter was a UH-1, the ubiquitous Huey, and its crew was made up of civilian soldiers. Lieutenant Arrigo Jezzi was one of the pilots. Sergeant John Healey and Sergeant Robert Yanacek were riding in back. The flight commander was the other pilot, Captain Lawrence Coyne.

It was a short flight, about a hundred-mile trip. The weather was clear, the night filled with stars.

Around 10:30 p.m., Sergeant Healey saw a red light off in the distance. Thinking it was just another aircraft, he didn't mention it to the others. A short while later, though, Sergeant Yanacek also saw the red light, and after watching it for a short while, finally mentioned it to Coyne. The commander calmly suggested he just keep an eye on it.

But then the light turned toward the Huey and started to grow rapidly in size. In seconds, it was heading for a collision with the helicopter.

Yanacek called out in alarm, and Coyne acted instantly. Taking over the controls, he put the Huey into a gut-wrenching dive, at the same time calling nearby Mansfield airfield on the radio. Coyne was convinced one of Mansfield's Air National Guard jet fighters was coming at him. But just as Coyne heard the first words of reply from the Mansfield ATC tower, the Huey's radio went dead. And still the red light was coming right at them, even as the Huey continued to dive.

The crew braced for a collision. The red light was right on them.

But then, suddenly, it just … stopped.

When the astonished crew finally opened their eyes, they saw a gray cigar-shaped craft right in front of them, flying in unison with the Huey. The craft was enormous.

The red light the copter crewmen had first spotted was on the craft's bow. There was a white light on its stern, and it had a green light underneath. A beam from this green light momentarily enveloped the copter's cockpit before shutting off.

The giant craft continued pacing them for about ten seconds. Then it took off at blinding speed, first heading west, then executing a sharp turn north before it finally blinked out.

Somehow Coyne regained control of the copter and was able to fly to a safe landing in Cleveland.

What makes this dramatic incident even more interesting was that there were ground witnesses as well. Follow-up research by ufologists located a woman and four youths who'd been driving in the area at the time of the incident. They reported seeing a bright red light flying over their heads at one point, but then lost sight of it.

The group continued driving and soon saw two bright lights, red and green. The driver pulled to the side of the road, and incredibly, the car's occupants witnessed the exact moment that the UFO had stopped in front of the Huey and began flying along with it. The five witnesses even reported seeing the green ray of light envelop the helicopter before the UFO sped off.

Many ufologists call the "Coyne Incident" one of the best UFO sightings ever.

Just Plain Crazy

Some stories are just too good to leave out.

George Washington and UFOs

What might be the strangest UFO story in U.S. military history — and there are many — is that George Washington may have encountered extraterrestrials during the dark days at Valley Forge.

This story comes from a Scottish researcher named Quentin Burde, who claims that in the winter of 1777-78, a tribe of Native-Americans whom Washington befriended while his exhausted and demoralized army was camped at Valley Forge were actually a group of green-skinned ETs.

Citing a reinterpretation of papers supposedly written by Washington's military secretary, Burde says he found references to "hovering lodges" and a tribe called the Greenskins who lived in a glowing globe in the woods nearby, a globe that was "sometimes there and sometimes not."

The Greenskins, Burde claims, provided the Continental Army with military intelligence and reconnaissance, and possibly advanced technology that helped turned the tide of the war.

Burde is quick to add, though, that he believes Washington had no idea he was dealing with creatures from another planet.

Rather, according to Burde, the man who would go on to win the Revolutionary War and become the first president of the United States probably thought he was talking with an "extremely talented Indian war chief, or a medicine man with powers bordering on the magical."

The Red Baron Incident

As the story goes, one day in the spring of 1917, with World War I raging across Western Europe, two Fokker triplanes of the German Air Force's *Jagdstaffel Jasta 11* took off from their base in occupied France and headed for the skies above Belgium. They were looking for Allied warplanes.

One of the Fokkers was piloted by Captain Peter Waitzrik; the other, by Captain Manfred von Richthofen, the famous Red Baron.

It was a clear morning, with few clouds and a bright blue sky. Von Richthofen was Germany's top fighter ace at the time. He'd already received the Blue Max, the country's highest military award, and within a month would be leading his legendary Red Baron's Flying Circus.

Not long into their patrol, Waitzrik and von Richthofen spotted something in the sky ahead of them. It was not an enemy fighter. According to Waitzrik, it was a flying object more than a hundred feet in diameter, bright silver in color and shaped like a saucer.

"We were terrified," Waitzrik said in an interview published years later. "We had never seen anything like it. But the United States had just entered the war, so we assumed it was something they'd sent up."

Von Richthofen immediately opened fire on the object, hitting it.

"The thing went down like a rock," Waitzrik said. "It sheared off tree limbs as it crashed in the woods."

Waitzrik and von Richthofen then watched as two occupants climbed out of the strange craft and escaped into the forest.

"The Baron and I gave a full report on the incident back at headquarters," Waitzrik said. "But they told us not to mention it ever again."

For years afterward, Waitzrik assumed the gleaming silver disk was some sort of Allied secret weapon — until the flying saucer craze of the late 1940s convinced him otherwise.

"That's when I realized this thing looked just like those saucer-shaped spaceships that everybody (started) seeing," Waitzrik said. "It's been many, many years now, so what difference could it possibly make? But there's no doubt in my mind (now) that it was no U.S. reconnaissance plane the Baron shot down that day. It was some kind of craft from another planet, and those guys who ran off into the woods weren't Americans."

Though he would shoot down a total of eighty Allied planes, von Richthofen would be dead within a year. Waitzrik survived the Great War and the next one and became an airline pilot.

About his encounter with the strange aerial craft, he confided years later: "Except for my wife and grandkids, I never told a soul."

D.C. = Demon Cat

The ghost of a giant black cat has been haunting Washington, D.C., for at least two centuries.

Described as being 12 feet long and ten feet high, the Demon Cat is said to be a ghostly survivor from the early 1800s when cats were intentionally released inside buildings in the nation's capital to kill mice.

Unsettlingly, the ethereal cat is usually seen before tragedies, as a harbinger of bad times to come.

In fact, White House security guards reportedly saw the phantom feline shortly before the Lincoln and Kennedy assassinations.

Giant Saves GI

Of all the reports of paranormal activity to come out of the Vietnam War, this might be the strangest.

One afternoon in late 1966, the witness in this odd incident was part of a U.S. Army helicopter force touching down in a landing zone close to the country's DMZ.

The communist enemy had opened up on the helicopters as they were landing. The American soldiers in the helicopters returned fire, and suddenly a full-scale battle was in progress.

Because the landing zone was covered with waist-high dry grass, several fires erupted as a result of the gunfire. Then one of the helicopters ran into trouble. Experiencing an engine malfunction on the ground, it was surrounded by the enemy and by grass fires.

The commanding officer of the landing force told the witness to grab a fire extinguisher from his helicopter and run back to the stricken one, hopefully to help rescue them.

The soldier did as ordered, taking the fire extinguisher but leaving his weapon behind. But once close to the damaged copter, he saw its crew waving him away — the engine problem had been fixed and the helicopter was taking off.

The soldier turned to return to his helicopter, but the smoke and flames from the grass fires, plus the firefight still going on around him, suddenly had him disoriented. In seconds, he was hopelessly lost.

Suddenly he heard someone yelling in Vietnamese. He turned to see an enemy soldier pointing his weapon at him. The American trooper, being unarmed, was sure his end was near.

Then he heard a loud crack and was certain he'd been shot, but felt no pain. Instead, he saw the enemy soldier fall to the ground, dead. That's when the U.S. soldier looked up to see an astonishing sight.

A figure at least eight feet tall was standing nearby. The creature was dressed "perfectly," in the witness's words, in a strange uniform with a sort of helmet covering most of his face. There was an aura around it, and somehow this giant had killed the enemy soldier and saved the American's life.

This creature was not of Earth yet it spoke to the American soldier, telling him all was okay and that he should return to his helicopter.

The soldier did as he was told and ran back to his copter unharmed.

As the copter took off, the man could see the dead enemy soldier, but there was no sign of the giant who'd saved his life.

Carrot-Top Aliens

One of America's strangest UFO incidents happened in Pascagoula, Mississippi.

On the night of October 11, 1973, two men fishing from a pier reported that a large cigar-shaped craft suddenly appeared in front of them. Three creatures emerged from the craft and abducted them. Described by both men as humanoid in shape, the creatures stood five feet tall, had lobster-like claws and only one leg.

Most unusual, though, there were three carrot-like growths on the creature's heads — one where a human's nose would be, and two where the ears would be.

The men say they were extensively probed by the creatures before finally being released.

Even More Weirdness from Real Life: The Original Face-for-Radio Story

I was a DJ for a few years at a small college radio station in upstate New York. We would do all kinds of crazy things. We used to give away free pizzas if two girls would come to the studio and kiss for ten seconds. We once had a beer drinking competition on the air. There was strip club nearby, and the dancers loved to be interviewed live.

We ran a contest called "Name That Food" where I'd read out the ingredients to the worst junk food imaginable and people would call in trying to guess what it was. We were very close to the Wilton Correctional Facility, so we pretended my radio sidekick, Mister Willy, was a murderer on work release from the prison.

The program following ours was a Grateful Dead show, and its DJ was a committed Dead Head who was very serious about the music. One night, just to goof on her, at the very end of our show, we announced that Jerry Garcia had passed away. When she came in for her show, we told her Jerry had died of a heart attack while jogging. It was all a joke to this point, and we didn't think she believed us.

But as soon as we left, she began to do a tear-filled tribute to Jerry … until someone called and told her she'd been punked. By that time so many people had heard her on the air that it wound up as a big story in one of the Albany newspapers.

The college eventually made us apologize to her on the air. The incident was brought up again a year later when they fired me.

Anyway, one night before a show, I stopped in a local drugstore to buy batteries. When I asked the woman behind the counter for a pack of double-As, she looked up at me and then put her hands over her eyes and said, "No — I can't look at you." I thought, what the eff is this? She said, "Are you the guy on the radio?" I said, "Yes." She said: "Oh, no — I can't look at you. I recognize your voice. I listen to you all the time. But you don't look anything like I thought you did!" She was almost crying. She got me the batteries and took my money, all while keeping one hand over her eyes. When she was done, she kind of waved me away. She never looked at me again.

I remember walking back to my car, stunned. Proof positive: I had a face for radio.

More Monster-Mania!

Altamaha-ha

Said to have the head of a crocodile and the long, thin body of a snake, this bizarre creature reportedly haunts the rivers of southeast Georgia. While Native Americans first reported seeing the beast hundreds of years ago, sightings continue today, mostly from people who encounter the Altamaha-ha while swimming.

Busco

As mentioned earlier, this monstrous turtle is said to live in a lake near Fort Wayne, Indiana. Spotted numerous times over the years, it measures six feet across, has a human-sized head and might weigh close to a ton.

Con Rit

One of the first recorded sightings of this sea monster came in 1899, when the crew of a British ship spotted one off the coast of Algeria. At least 150 feet long with hundreds of fast-moving fins and a lobster-like tail, the immense creature kept pace with the ship for more than a half hour.

Dobhar-Chu

This creature is said to dwell in a number of Irish lakes. Also known as "the Irish crocodile," it looks like a cross between gigantic otter and a greyhound. Legends say the Dobhar-Chu is so dangerous, just glimpsing it will cause instant death.

Emela-Ntouka

This rhino-like creature reportedly lives in the rivers of the African Congo. Bigger than an elephant with a tail like a crocodile, it has a single large horn protruding from its head. These animals can become so violent when agitated, they've been known to disembowel elephants.

Flathead Monster

This serpent-like creature haunts Montana's Flathead Lake. More than 15 feet long and four feet around, it displays three distinct humps when swimming on the surface. Many fishermen report seeing the monster taking fish right off their hooks.

Gloucester Sea Monster

In the summer of 1817, hundreds of people in the seaport town of Gloucester, Massachusetts, saw a 100-foot-long sea monster swimming through their harbor. Witnesses, who described it as having large eyes and rows of sharp teeth, flocked to the seashore to catch sight of the beast.

Cryptozoologists point out that because Gloucester is a large fishing community with residents familiar with all types of sea creatures, this one must have been unusual, indeed.

Hoop Snake

This weird creature has been reported in Minnesota, Wisconsin, North Carolina, and even parts of Australia. A highly poisonous predator, the snake grasps its tail with its jaws and, by creating a "hoop," rolls after its prey at high speed, straightening out at the last second to impale its victim with its venom-filled tail.

Issie

In 1978, two dozen witnesses attending a family get-together on the Japanese island of Kyushu spotted this strange creature in a nearby lake. Described as reptilian with jet-black skin, according to one witness, it was nearly a 100 feet long and displayed humps rising two feet above the lake's surface while swimming.

Jersey Devil

Born in 1735 to a cursed family living in New Jersey's Pine Barrens, this horrible-looking creature attacked its mother at the moment of birth before escaping up a chimney. Dubbed the Jersey Devil, the monstrous toddler has been terrorizing the Pine Barrens ever since.

Kongamato

This flying animal, seen throughout southern Africa, is either a gigantic bat or possibly a pterodactyl left over from the Jurassic age. First spotted by Western scientists in 1923, it has a wingspan of 10 feet, a long, narrow tail, and a mouthful of sharp teeth. For some reason, Kongamatos attack anyone who is in or near the water.

Lusca

Andros Island, the largest island in the Bahamas, is not only home to the Navy's Area 51, but reportedly this weird creature as well. Resembling a real-life Sharktopus, with multiple arms and shark-like features, it inhabits the island's deep-water caverns, known as Blue Holes. Luscas will attack anything that comes near them, making recreational diving around Andros extremely risky.

Megalodon

Thought extinct for more than a million years, one of these gigantic prehistoric sharks, described as at least 100 feet long, was spotted by a group of fishermen off New

Zealand in 1918. Several more sightings of this "Super-Jaws" monster have been reported since.

Nandi Bear

Descriptions of this huge East African animal vary. Some witnesses say it's a cross between a bear and a hyena. Others claim that, with a thick mane, long claws, and large teeth, it resembles a monstrous baboon. Either way, it's an extremely dangerous animal that eats humans and livestock alike.

Owlman

Described as an owl the size of a man, this winged creature was first spotted in mid-1976, hovering over Mawnan Church in Cornwall, England. A couple of months later, more witnesses saw it again near the same church. Other sightings followed. Some investigators speculate that because Mawnan Church is built atop a ley line, the Owlman might be a manifestation of some unexplained energy surrounding the building.

Pope Lick Monster

This creature haunts a particular railroad trestle near Louisville, Kentucky, luring people to cross it only to have them killed by fast-moving trains. Said to resemble a grotesquely deformed man with transparent skin, the monster is able to mimic the voices of loved ones, which helps it entice unsuspecting victims to their deaths.

Queensland Tiger

Well known to Australian aborigines, this huge cat with stripes across half its back has a nasty habit of using its razor-like claws to rip out the stomachs of its prey — which includes kangaroos and humans — before devouring them.

Ropen

First spotted in remote parts of Papua, New Guinea, this creature is said to be a cross between a giant bat and a pterosaur, a flying dinosaur long thought to be extinct. Seen only after dark, the Ropen has the ability to light up at night through some form of bioluminescence. While most accounts say it lives on fish, there are also reports of it feasting on human corpses pulled from recently dug graves. It's possibly the model for the famous movie monster, Rodan.

Shug Monkey

This creature is said to have the head and body of an ape but the legs, feet, and paws of a large mastiff-like dog. First reported by Vikings settling in the British Isles around 1000 A.D., Shug Monkeys are still reported today.

As recently as 2009, three witnesses spotted one not far from Rendlesham Forest, the site of one of the most spectacular UFO sightings in history.

Turtle Lake Monster

This cryptid inhabits Turtle Lake in West Saskatchewan, Canada. Thirty feet long with a head that resembles a pig, the beast is sighted on average about twice a year. Locals tell of people going near the lake and being snapped up, never to be seen again. One theory says the monster is a prehistoric plesiosaur left over from the days when Saskatchewan was the site of a large freshwater sea.

Urayuli

Said to inhabit the forests of southwestern Alaska, these Yeti-like creatures stand more than 10 feet tall, have long, shaggy fur and weirdly luminescent eyes. They can emit a high-pitched cry that frightens animals and humans alike. Local legends say the Urayuli are children who became lost in the woods at night and were later transformed into monsters.

Vampire Squid

This bizarre creature has huge black eyes and a bright red cloak that connects its eight arms. The only squid that does not to hunt living prey, it feasts on dead creatures found at the bottom of the ocean.

Werewolf

For centuries, tales about some humans having the ability to turn into wolf-like creatures were simply considered myths. But a recent book documents dozens of eyewitness accounts of actual werewolf sightings around the U.S., with New Jersey topping the list.

X-Monster

Said to be a cross between a vampire and troll, this beast attacks travelers along a road in Serbia known as the X highway, draining its victims of blood and then eating them whole.

Yowie

This Down Under ape-like creature has a human-like face, long canine teeth, and makes a horrendous sound if frightened. Like Florida's Skunk Ape, the Yowie also emits a terrible smell.

Zuiyo-Maru Monster

In April 1977, the crew of a Japanese fishing boat found a huge unidentifiable carcass floating off the coast of New Zealand. Thirty-three feet long and weighing more than two tons, it had a snakelike head at the end of a long, slender neck. After studying photos of the carcass, Japanese scientists theorized the creature might have been the descendent of the plesiosaur, a gigantic prehistoric beast.

Brave New World: Part 2

Fifteen good reasons to head for the hills…

1. Big Brother 1

The National Security Agency is America's largest and, until recently, its most secret intelligence agency.

The NSA employs at least 50,000 people, twice as many as the CIA. Basically a gigantic eavesdropping operation, it intercepts more than a billion telephone and internet communications around the world every day.

It also scoops ups millions of contact lists from email and instant messaging accounts globally on a daily basis. Way back in 2012, media reports said the NSA collected nearly a half-million email address books, including more than 100,000 from Hotmail, 80,000 from Facebook, and 30,000 from Gmail — in a single day.

If you were using any of those services back then — or if you still are now — there's a good chance the NSA is snooping on you.

2. Big Brother 2

The NSA commands fleets of orbiting satellites, operates massive eavesdropping stations worldwide, and employs a vast army of internet geeks to do its dirty work.

But it has also developed many ordinary-looking devices to spy on you. For instance, media reports have revealed the NSA invented a USB cable, the kind used in just about every computer in America, that has an almost invisible radio transceiver hidden inside it.

These cables are rumored to be in wide circulation and could be hooked up anywhere — maybe even inside your own home.

3. Big Brother 3

The NSA also has software, called DROPOUTJEEP, that allows it to not just monitor but actually *control* all the features on your smart phone, including its geolocation function, its text messaging system, and its microphone and camera.

4. Through the Keyhole

There is an infamous U.S. spy satellite called the Keyhole-11.

Controlled by the U.S. military, its cameras are so powerful, experts claim that from 125 five miles up, the Keyhole can count the number of buttons on your shirt, tell the brand of shoes you wear, and see the time on your wristwatch.

What's frightening about this is that the Keyhole has been doing these things since 1976.

Vastly updated versions are in orbit today, with as many as six going over our heads at any given moment. This begs the question: What can Keyhole see these days?

5. What's Bugging You?

The Intelligence Advanced Research Projects Activity, or IARPA, is a little known U.S. intelligence agency that builds spy equipment beyond Ian Fleming's wildest dreams.

Though the vast majority of IARPA's inventions are highly classified, media sources have revealed that the agency has created flocks of robotic birds, flying insects, and other winged creatures that can carry tiny microphones and cameras for spying on unsuspecting NSA targets.

These animatronic spy drones are said to be virtually indistinguishable from the real things, so if the next fly you swat goes crunch, you'll know why.

6. My Chevy the Spy

Many new cars now come equipped with data collection devices also known as black boxes.

Similar to those found inside airplanes, these boxes record such things as how fast you drive, how much force you use on the gas pedal, how quickly you brake, and if you negotiate corners in an aggressive manner.

In event of an accident, your insurance company can access this information, ostensibly to determine fault. But they can also use the data to judge if you're a safe driver or not.

If the black box says you're not driving the way the insurance company thinks you should, your rates will probably go up, or you might be dropped altogether.

7. Dirty Coppers?

Recent media reports say that police departments across the United States are amassing enormous amounts of personal information on law-abiding citizens — and doing so without old-fashioned warrants.

Instead, they are collecting people's cellphone data by not only tapping into cellphone towers, but even creating fake towers that act as data traps.

8. Do It Yourself

Maybe it's paranoia or just human nature, but with so many revelations about government spying in recent years, sales of affordable spy gadgets for ordinary citizens have skyrocketed.

Mini spy cameras and microphones hidden in such mundane items as pens, baseball caps, coat hooks, alarm clocks, smoke detectors, eyeglasses, thumb drives, water bottles, books, ordinary-looking rocks and more can now be bought online, cheaply and with no questions asked.

9. Nasal Drip

Sufferers of chronic nasal congestion will know this drill.

Every time they purchase an over-the-counter medication to relieve their ailment, they must show a picture ID, which is then scanned and its personal information sent to a tracking database called the National Precursor Log Exchange.

The reason is that many anti-congestion medications contain ingredients that can be used in making methamphetamine, and repeated purchases act as a red flag for law enforcement agencies.

But even though only a tiny percentage of people buying these legal medications intend to use them to cook meth, every customer is tracked and their information is stored forever.

10. Trust No Avatar

According to documents leaked by whistleblower Edward Snowden a few years ago, the NSA routinely spies on the worldwide online gaming community.

For instance, the agency has the capability to scoop up massive amounts of data within the Xbox Live console network, used by more than 48 million players.

What's more, real-life NSA agents disguised as ordinary players are lurking inside virtual reality sites such as World of Warcraft and Second Life to further spy on you.

While the NSA says it's doing this because it believes terrorists can use these sites to plan attacks, everyone is caught up in their snoop traps — something to think about the next time you do the cyber nasty with Lucinda the Troll under the Bridge of Souls.

11. You Can Bank On It

While the NSA is the *uber* boogey man when it comes to spying, your local bank might not be much better.

Because of the explosion of inexpensive surveillance equipment, bank lobbies now contain more cameras than the set of a Hollywood blockbuster.

More disturbing, some large banks have changed their depositor agreement terms to allow them to secretly track customers via social media. Other banks can store your image, recordings of your voice, and transactions on your account — all because, so they say, they can better learn which of their services and products you might want to purchase in the future.

In other words, sell you stuff you probably don't want or need.

12. Spy Blimps

Sometime in the near future, if not already, the U.S. Government is expected to deploy a fleet of spy blimps capable of tracking individuals from more than 12 miles up.

Powered by solar cells, these secret airships will be able to stay aloft for up to ten years. Plus, unlike orbiting satellites which are overhead for only short periods of time, the blimps will be able to hover over one place or even one person for very long periods of time.

Though originally designed for use over battlefields, experts say the secret inflatables will also be able to float over major U.S. cities without anyone knowing it.

13. Drone-On Amazon

When Amazon first announced plans to use drones to make deliveries, aviation and privacy experts were alarmed.

The fear is that not only could hundreds of Amazon drones flying around pose a public safety hazard, but that the company's delivery vehicles could also double as information-gathering devices.

The same drone that delivers your new book could also take a picture of your car, your deck furniture, the kind of windows you have on your house, or even the clothes you wear — and then secretly sell that invaluable information to ravenous marketers.

14. Death by Toaster

Just about all spy gear is run by microchips these days, and the smaller and more powerful the chip, the more insidious the device can be. Experts say that in the very near future, "chip power" will be nearly forty times greater than it is at present.

This will have huge impact on what's called "the Internet of Things," in which many of the inanimate objects that surround us — appliances, vehicles, food products, clothing, buildings and machines — will contain chips and will be connected to one big network.

Not only does this raise the possibility that these everyday objects could be turned into spy devices, they also could become weapons for assassination.

If the NSA identifies a potential terrorist, or maybe just someone it doesn't like, the brakes on that person's car might suddenly fail. Or their airplane's engines might mysteriously stop working. Or one of their household appliances might suddenly electrocute them.

15. Tattoo You?

Futurists predict that within a few years there will be an app that will allow anyone to see everything you've ever done in your digital life.

Your so-called "digital tattoo" contains every action you've ever taken online, past and present, including every email, tweet and Facebook posting, every website you've ever visited, every document or photo you've ever downloaded, every Skype chat you've ever had, on and on. And the reason it's called a tattoo is that the information it contains can never, ever be delated.

Special Considerations

<u>Ong's Hat</u>

New Jersey's Pine Barrens can be found near one of the most densely populated parts of the United States.

The heavily wooded expanse of coastal plain is close to New York City, Philadelphia, and Atlantic City. The Garden State Parkway, the most heavily-traveled toll road in the U.S., runs right through it. Yet few people are aware this 1,500-square-mile forest even exists.

The Pine Barrens are almost devoid of people. Early settlers found the sugar-like soil impossible to work with and moved on. But when it comes to the paranormal, the place is almost overcrowded.

Start with the aforementioned New Jersey Devil. Described as having the body of a serpent, the head of a horse, the wings of a bat, and a devil's forked tail, this creature has been haunting the Pine Barrens since the mid-1700s. Then there's the monstrous black dog that's said to roam the forest, consuming anything that crosses its path. A spirit called the Golden Haired Girl hides in the woods, looking forlornly toward the sea, forever waiting for her drowned lover to return. A ghostly deer known as the White Stag is said to lead travelers lost in the Barrens to safety. And on stormy nights, the notorious Captain Kidd, who buried some of his treasure in the Barrens, can be seen walking a nearby beach, minus his head.

The Pine Barrens also have their own ghost town. Little more than a tavern and a few small buildings at the intersection of two dirt roads, it was home in the late 1870s to a man named Jacob Ong. One night he somehow got his hat stuck in a tree outside the tavern. It remained entangled in the branches for so long the place became known as Ong's Hat.

By the 1920s, all traces of the tiny village had disappeared and it became little more than an odd name in the middle of this odd, out-of-place wilderness.

But many believe it was here that a small group of scientists did nothing less than open a door to another dimension.

Twins Frank and Althea Dobbs were raised on a UFO-cult commune in rural Texas. Growing up in the 1960s, they attended the University of Texas as physics majors. It was here that they developed a series of radical theories they believed would allow humans to travel to other dimensions.

Enrolled at Princeton University in the mid-'80s, the twins submitted a thesis on interdimensional travel called

Cognitive Chaos — and were immediately expelled. Determined to prove their theory, they bought an old Airstream trailer, drove it to Ong's Hat, constructed a crude laboratory inside it, and went back to work.

More scientists soon joined the twins in their unusual studies, and a small commune of admirers grew up around Ong's Hat. After just three years, the group had created a device they called "the Gate." On one side was the old trailer; on the other, another dimension.

The scientists built a capsule to travel through the Gate, and a commune member volunteered to be its first passenger. As predicted by the twins' theories, the capsule vanished from the laboratory only to reappear seven minutes later, its passenger still safe inside.

The volunteer reported that he'd found himself in a place exactly like the Pine Barrens, in a world exactly like Earth, with one exception: There were no humans. Subsequent trips confirmed it. The new dimension was just like this one, just with no people.

Even though as time went by the commune members visited more dimensions, they always kept a soft spot for this first place. They set up an alternate colony in this "second" Pine Barrens and began spending most of their time there, coming back to our present dimension only to get necessities. But they never intended to leave this world behind. They considered themselves travelers; they liked going back and forth.

Then something went wrong.

Either prodded by intelligence that the group had something to do with a dangerous chemical leak at nearby Fort Dix, or possibly tipped to their bizarre activities, the U.S. Army's Delta Force stormed Ong's Hat in force. In an action eerily similar to the Waco Branch Davidian raid, the commune was burned to the ground, and up to seven residents were either killed or went missing. The settlement was bulldozed, and the Ong's Hat commune was eliminated for good.

Yet why was none of this ever reported in the media?

Maybe because none of it ever happened.

But please read on.

It's widely believed that the story of the Ong's Hat commune was created in the early 1990s by author Joseph Matheny to start the first myth on the then-budding World Wide Web. Matheny and his friends planted pieces of the tale on early internet bulletin boards, disguising them as true items. Incredibly, others began responding to the postings with their own details about the Ong's Hat commune. Some of these responses even included arti-facts such as videotapes and sound recordings.

Matheny's original story grew like an extremely elaborate kids' game of telephone — and that's how cyberspace's first legend was born: not by numerous retellings around a campfire, but by numerous retellings on the internet.

But ... because the story of Ong's Hat induced so many extraordinary responses from so many participants, thousands of people came to believe the story was true, and in some eyes, this alone *made* it true. There is a theory, complex and still unproven, that strange things exist in our world — ghosts, monsters, aliens — simply because so many people think about them and believe in them. This alone gives them life. In other words, if enough people think something is true, then it *must* be true.

Whatever the reason, even though some reports say Matheny called the story to a halt in 2001, hardcore believers still travel to the Pine Barrens, hoping to find (and maybe finding) the interdimensional portal at Ong's Hat.

Rosslyn

As mentioned earlier, more UFOs have been reported around the Scottish Midlands village of Bonnybridge than anywhere else on Earth.

The British government received *three thousand* UFO reports from Bonnybridge in just the second half of the 1990s. More than half of the village's 6000 residents have seen a UFO; many have seen more than one. People have reported giant UFOs landing in fields just outside the village, air traffic controllers at nearby airports have tracked UFOs moving at impossible speeds, and airline pilots have encountered bizarre flashing lights during takeoffs and landings.

Bonnybridge lies within the Falkirk Triangle, an area that stretches from Stirling in the north down to Glasgow and parts south of Edinburgh. The Triangle is well known to UFO researchers for its many unexplained aerial sightings over the years and, for whatever reason, Bonnybridge happens to be in the thick of this perplexing activity.

But Bonnybridge is not the only place in the Midlands where bizarre things happen. About forty miles east of Bonnybridge is the rural village of Gorebridge. Located deep within the Falkirk Triangle, with a population of about 5000, Gorebridge boasts its fair share of UFO incidents as well. In recent years, people have reported seeing spherical shapes, triangle shapes, black flying orbs, and bright orange globes flying overhead or hovering above the town. Numerous witnesses have also seen UFOs flying in formation over the area.

But this is just the beginning of the strangeness. Black helicopters are frequently seen flying above Gorebridge. Residents report meeting people they describe as Men in Black walking in the local woods. There's an abandoned coal mine nearby that's known for attracting lights in the night sky and drawing them down to it. In the 18th century, residents of Gorebridge saw "a city" descending from the sky and landing nearby. The Roman Ninth Legion, a 5,000-man army stationed in the Gorebridge area during the Roman occupation, simply disappeared one day, never to be seen again. Near Crichton Castle there's a place called Valley of the Bones, where locals say werewolves are frequently seen and heard howling. There are also many ghosts reportedly haunting the castle itself.

So Gorebridge *is* a very unusual place. But it gets even weirder …

Not far from Gorebridge there's an old church called Rosslyn Chapel.

The chapel is at once fascinating and puzzling. Its exterior features the standard Gothic gargoyles and flying buttresses, but inside there are some bizarre pillar carvings, a baffling ceiling design, many unexplainable "music boxes" in the walls, and more than 100 so-called Green Men, creatures set into the masonry that have plant life coming out of their mouths.

But the strangest thing about Rosslyn Chapel is not its odd interior but rather who built it and why.

Though it's a topic not without controversy, there are many researchers of both medieval history and paranormal studies who are convinced that this chapel, built in this very odd place, has a direct connection to the infamous Knights Templar.

The Templars were an order of warrior monks created in France in 1118 to protect religious pilgrims traveling to the holy lands of the Middle East. Though they started off as penniless bodyguards working for scraps, their fame and fortune grew fast. In very little time, the Templars became immensely wealthy, politically powerful, and much feared militarily throughout Europe and the Middle East — and they stayed that way for more than 150 years.

But eventually they became too powerful, so on October 13, 1307 (a Friday, making "Friday the thirteenth" a universally unlucky day), King Philip IV of France had many of the Templars arrested. Falsely charged with crimes against the crown, hundreds were tortured and burned at the stake.

However, it's believed many more Templars were able to escape to parts unknown, taking their tremendous wealth with them. Maybe one of those places was the Scottish Midlands.

Rosslyn Chapel was built in the fifteenth century, more than 150 years after the Templars disappeared. However, some researchers insist the chapel's builder, William Sinclair, was somehow involved with the Knights, pointing to what they consider to be Templar clues that Sinclair put all over the interior of the small church.

For instance, only one Latin inscription can be found inside the chapel. Translated, it reads, "Wine is strong, a king is stronger, females are stronger still, but truth conquers everything." This phrase was first uttered by the man who built the Temple of Solomon in Jerusalem, the *same place* that, centuries later, became the field headquarters of the Knights Templar.

Another carving inside the chapel shows two men riding the same horse. This image is so closely associated with the Templars that it appears on their coat of arms.

Many claim that a grave on the chapel grounds marked "William Sinclair, Knight Templar" is that of the builder. One of the Templars' signature eight-point crosses is carved into the gravestone.

Beneath the floor of Rosslyn Chapel, though, is said to be the biggest mystery of all: a massive underground vault, sealed in 1690, that has never been reopened. No one knows what's down there, but at least one legend says a dozen Knights Templar are buried in full armor within.

One of the pillars inside the church, called the Prentice Pillar, is ornately carved with coiled spirals that look exactly like the double helix of DNA. Is it just a fluke that hundreds of years later, just down the road at the Roslin Institute, Dolly the sheep would become the world's first DNA animal clone?

Botanists have also confirmed that there are depictions of sweet corn and cactus in the chapel masonry. The trouble is, these plants were indigenous to South America and thus unknown in Europe at the time the chapel was built.

Many of the chapel's arches contain what people call "music boxes," square protrusions that, by their numbers and placement, seem to present some kind of code, possibly one based on the musical scales. But this code has yet to be broken.

At the top of the chapel's ceiling is the so-called Great Rose Window. At noon on the days of the summer and winter solstices, a ray of light strikes this piece of glass directly and bathes the entire interior in a blood-red light.

This seems like a lot of mystery and intrigue for what is basically a small country chapel. So why was this odd church built here in the first place? Is it just a coincidence that a place of worship with such a close connection to the mysterious Templars is located in an area that's now considered the world's leading hot spot for UFO sightings?

The area around Gorebridge has been described as a "thin place," a location where the unusual is the usual, where the line between the possible and the impossible doesn't exist. With that in mind, we'll end on one last very unusual thing about Gorebridge.

People who live in this area — where UFO sightings are commonplace, werewolves can be heard screaming at night, ghosts roam free, and entire armies simply disappear — also win the British National Lottery more than anyone else in the United Kingdom.

The M-Triangle

Six hundred miles east of Moscow in a remote region of Russia near the Ural Mountains is a place called the Perm Anomalous Zone.

Better known as the M-Triangle, the area encompasses 40 square miles of mostly mountainous terrain along the Silva River, near the village of Molebka. And according to the locals, like the Falkirk section of Scotland, strange things have been happening there for hundreds of years.

Bizarre lights in the woods, unexplained craft streaking overhead, encounters with otherworldly beings, even weird symbols and letters written across the sky. Something highly unusual is said to occur inside the Triangle almost every day, and reportedly, many times, dozens of weird things are going on there at once.

As is almost always the case, the strangeness begins with UFOs, and in this instance, brightly lit ones. Witnesses say they come in many colors and shapes, including spheres, domes, and saucers. Sometimes these objects fly over the Triangle; sometimes they hover above it. But they've also been seen in the woods themselves, floating low to the ground, moving in and out of the trees like phantoms. So many UFOs are spotted around the M-Triangle that a large wooden statue has been erected in the village of Molebka to commemorate these otherworldly visitors.

Other bizarre things happen inside the M-Triangle as well. A research group camping deep in the woods heard the sound of a car driving toward them, an impossibility due to the thickness of the forest. Another team heard strange voices from dusk to dawn, voices so clear and distinct they seemed just a few feet away. A ghostly whistle, an electrical buzzing noise, and the sound of ancient choral singing are also frequently reported inside the zone.

Fire behaves very peculiarly inside the Triangle. Researchers have reported instances in which a flame of any size will suddenly explode, as if being fed by an invisible propellant. Scientists have no clue why this occurs.

Then there is the Call Box. There's virtually no cell phone service inside the Triangle, except at one place researchers have dubbed the Call Box. A person who stands inside this five-foot-square piece of ground, for some unknown reason, can make a cellphone call to anywhere in the world.

Time seems distorted inside the Triangle. One of the first group of researchers to go into the area in 1990 reported each member's electronic watch stopped at precisely the same moment and began flashing 00:00. Other researchers said that in some places their watches would show a time hours ahead of the actual time, while in others, watches run hours behind.

And many researchers who have gone into the Triangle report that it's impossible to shake the feeling that someone is watching you at all times.

The M-Triangle wasn't very well-known until the late 1980s. Up to then, the old hardline Soviet government had forbidden journalists from reporting or writing anything about UFOs, and that included the unusual activity around Molebka. Civilian access to the area was nearly impossible, and although Moscow sent several expeditions into the region over the years, what they found was never disclosed.

The crumbling Soviet government finally removed the ban in 1988, and many researchers jumped at the chance to study the strange place. A few civilian expeditions finally went in, and their reports caused a sensation when they reached the world media in 1989. Research groups have been visiting the Triangle ever since.

But Russia being Russia, even these days, researchers claim the entire area is under constant surveillance by the FSB, the Kremlin's intelligence agency and successor to the KGB.

Valery Yakimov, director of the Ural-UFO group, has had extensive experiences inside the M-Triangle, and his excursions have produced some fantastic observations.

One night, Yakimov and his research group saw what they described as an unusually shaped sky. The stars directly over their heads became so concentrated it was as if they were forming a dome. Yet all other parts of the sky appeared completely normal.

On another occasion, Yakimov's team saw up to two dozen stars moving in what he described as inconceivable trajectories. The stars floated over the researchers' heads and formed a gigantic circle above them. They saw this vision on four consecutive nights, always just after midnight. On another expedition, Yakimov's group observed a number of strange geometrical shapes — squares and triangles mostly -- floating through the forest. Varying from silver to white to bright blue, the shapes would remain visible until someone tried to get close to them, at which point they would disappear. And though dozens of people saw them, the shapes could not be caught on film or video.

During yet another expedition into the Triangle, Yakimov's team saw many mysterious spheres gliding over the area. These objects were either white or orange, with diameters ranging from three to ten feet. Usually spotted in groups of three to five, the spheres would slowly approach the scientific team and float over their heads, or sometimes briefly hover above the group, before moving on. It was almost as if they were observing Yakimov and his crew, just as the researchers were observing them.

Another M-Triangle expert, Nikolay Subbotin, director of the Russian UFO Research Station, was camped out for the night deep inside the Triangle when he and his team spotted a brilliant ray of light rising into the sky from behind a grove of trees. An instant later, a second ray appeared, parallel to the first. Both slowly began to move in opposite directions, lighting up the area all around them.

Subbotin and his friends watched this extravaganza for about 15 minutes before being distracted by another incredible display. The clouds over their heads, formerly cumulus and puffy, suddenly lined up into a lattice formation, five vertical and five horizontal stripes, stretching across the sky.

They stayed this way for nearly a half hour before finally disappearing.

Other people entering the Triangle report events more down to Earth, though no less amazing.

A husband-and-wife team visiting the area for the first time soon became aware of a strange buzzing noise all around them. They described it as sounding like a water pump.

They heard it no matter where they went, no matter what direction they were heading. This was the case for their entire visit. When the couple returned to the Triangle later that year, the noise was still audible.

This same couple noticed odd things about the area's animal life as well. While wading in shallow waters of a river, they observed that fish had no qualms about swimming right up to them and eating food out of their hands. Butterflies and dragonflies would also frequently land on them and stay in place, totally unafraid of human contact.

But apparently there are other creatures roaming around the zone, ones this world is not so familiar with. Glowing ETs and other nonhumans have been frequently reported in the area. Some of the latter, known locally as Snow People, perfectly fit the description of Bigfoot. Others have even more bizarre appearances.

Valery Yakimov says his most chilling M-Triangle encounter involved meeting one of these alien beings face to face. It happened during an expedition in which Yakimov had brought into the Triangle some people who had never been there before. Yakimov took the rookies to a spot where researchers say they usually feel a presence of "the unknown." At that point, it was suggested that the group split up and walk about one at a time. This way the newcomers would be able to experience the full intensity of the M-Triangle.

While walking alone, Yakimov was confronted by a creature almost nine feet tall and black in color. Yakimov turned and ran, eventually reuniting with his group. A short time later, one of his team members reported she'd had a meeting with a strange being as well, yet this one she described as a little green man, about three feet tall.

Another story relayed by Nikolay Subbotin told of a researcher camping out in the Triangle who went to collect some water. Walking back to camp, he realized someone was following him. He immediately began to run, but not before getting a good look at his stalker, which sounds close in description to the being Yakimov had encountered.

"The creature walked slowly," the researcher recalled. "It was black, with white stuff on its body. It wore a kind of skin tight skirt and was about nine feet tall. The eyes were large and shiny and it had long arms."

Why is the M-Triangle the way it is? There are rumors that a secret weapons facility is located somewhere beneath the zone. This would account for the constant electrical sounds heard there, as well as reports of Russian soldiers often seen in the area. It would also explain why the place is of such interest to Russia's intelligence agencies.

There are also stories about past attempts at mining strontium in the area. Strontium is an earth metal that's used to block X-rays in old tube TV sets. Other UFO researchers theorize that uranium found in the nearby mountains might be attracting UFOs. Some have even speculated the presence of this uranium causes mass hallucinations in the zone.

Subbotin had heard that in the 1950s and '60s, a highly classified underground test laboratory inside the Triangle had conducted secret experiments into large electromagnetic fields. Supposedly something went wrong in the course of these experiments, and everyone involved had to be evacuated from the area. The underground laboratory was then flooded as a safety measure.

But these theories are speculation. No solid reason has ever been given as to why things are the way they are inside the Triangle, or why local villagers say strange things have been happening there for centuries.

But what *really* makes the M-Triangle different is the astonishing personal effect it has on many of the people who go into the area.

While there have been stories of some being adversely affected within the Triangle — burns, confusion, even reports of a suicide -- more often, the tales are about how a person's well-being vastly improves after a trip inside.

There have been reports of people with serious medical issues visiting the M-Triangle and coming out cured. And many healthy people leave feeling what one Russian researcher called "a general improvement in all spheres." Not only do people report feeling better physically and mentally after being inside the Triangle, they also say they feel different *spiritually* and *morally*.

One researcher wrote, "The drawbacks of one's character seem to disappear here; the good intentions and high feelings come to life."

There's also a kind of creative effect that reportedly infuses some people who spend time in the Triangle. Abilities become sharper; previously unknown talents come to the fore.

There is one story in particular that seems to underscore to even the most skeptical person that something extremely unusual is happening inside the M-Triangle.

It is the story of Pavel Mukhortov. Discharged from the Soviet Army in the 1980s for health reasons and for a time unemployed, Mukhortov eventually found work as a journalist. He'd heard about strange things going on inside the M-Triangle and considered visiting the place to see for himself, but he wasn't sure. However, when he learned the KGB was continuously monitoring the area, Mukhortov found the impetus he needed. He joined a research party and set off to explore the area.

Immediately on arrival, Mukhortov sensed something eerie about in the place. While some members of his group soon fell sick, Mukhortov found himself enveloped by uncontrollable emotions.

Photos of strange flying objects were taken during this expedition, and according to a *People* magazine article from October 1989, Mukhortov claimed to have met and spoken with an alien while inside the Triangle.

But the *really* strange stuff started happening once Mukhortov left and returned to Moscow. Soon after arriving in the Russian capital, the reporter began to feel radically different. Hardly a genius when he went on his trip to the Triangle, he suddenly found himself saturated with knowledge about aerospace physics — something he'd been completely unfamiliar with previously.

Incredibly, he'd become *so* enlightened in this area that he eventually applied for and was accepted to the Russian space program. He became a cosmonaut a short time later.

A place where the unusual is usual. Where people become enlightened spiritually. Where the universe chooses to reveal incredible stellar displays. Where animals have no fear of humans, and where beings not like us walk about freely.

Where diseases are cured and people turn more righteous, and where an ordinary man can be enlightened enough to master the secrets of outer space.

No one knows why these things happen in the M-Triangle and nowhere else. But if there's such a thing as heaven on Earth, this place might be it.

About the Author

Mack Maloney has written more than 50 books, including *"UFOs in Wartime – What They Didn't Want You To Know"* and *"Beyond Area 51,"* plus the best-selling *"Wingman"* military adventure series. He's served as a consultant for a government-funded research firm working with U.S. intelligence agencies and is a member of the rock band, "Sky Club."

Coming Soon!

A NEW SERIES FROM
BEST-SELLING AUTHOR

Mack Maloney

A Codename Starman Adventure
Book I

The Kalashnikov Kiss

For more information
visit Mack at:

www.speakingvolumes.us

Coming Spring 2019

The Odessa Raid
Book 19
in
Mack Maloney's Best-Selling

Wingman Series

The sequel to Battle for America, Wingman leads an air strike
on a secret Arctic base belonging to super-terrorist Viktor
Robotov only to find his way back to America filled with bizarre twists and turns.

For more information
visit Mack at:

www.speakingvolumes.us

Sign up for free and bargain books

Join the Speaking Volumes mailing list

Text

ILOVEBOOKS

to 22828 to get started.

Printed in Great Britain
by Amazon

74516273R00192